Maps & Models

FOR MINISTRY

Edited by

DAVID WHITELAW

POINT LOMA
PRESS

SAN DIEGO, CALIFORNIA

Maps and Models for Ministry
Copyright ©1996 by Wesleyan Center Books, a division of Point Loma Press,
the publishing extension of Point Loma Nazarene College, San Diego, Calif.

*PLNC's Wesleyan Center for Twenty-First Century Studies has been created
to inspire a new generation of Wesleyan thinking that will influence the
broader church and social worlds of the twenty-first century.*

Please address any comments or questions to:
Wesleyan Center for Twenty-First Century Studies
Point Loma Nazarene College
3900 Lomaland Drive
San Diego CA 92106
or e-mail: wesleyancenter@ptloma.edu

ISBN: 0-9652698-1-7
Printed in the United States of America.

Editor: David Whitelaw
Cover Design: Michelle Shoemaker
Book Design: Stella Vandegrift

CONTENTS

ACKNOWLEDGEMENTS

In a work such as this, with seventeen contributing writers, it is impossible to acknowledge all who have been of assistance in the development, compilation, and publication of this manuscript. However, there are a few to whom we are especially indebted and must give personal thanks.

I express my thanks to Janine Metcalf and Steve Rodeheaver, who faithfully served on the book committee and worked tirelessly through a multitude of meetings to attend to all the details that a project such as this generates.

Sincere thanks also go to Sharon Bowles, Karen DeSollar and Stella Vandegrift who accepted additional responsibilities to format, proofread, and prepare the text for publication.

Dr. Maxine Walker, director for the Wesleyan Center for Twenty-First Century Studies and Point Loma Press, has been a guiding light in bringing this work from its early stages to actual publication. Her encouragement and direction have been vital to the project.

I also thank the Wesleyan Center for funding this work and the staff of Point Loma Press for their fine editorial and marketing efforts. Their commitment to excellence is evident and much appreciated.

I am especially grateful to Darlene Forward who has been of tremendous help in preparing the final manuscript for submission to Point Loma Press. Her editorial skills, willingness to help as needed, and efficiency in compiling the contributions on one disk have been invaluable. She has been grace to this project.

The reader may find the concepts of Dr. Frank G. Carver's chapter expanded in chapters 6, 9, and 10 of *When Jesus Said Good-bye.* Copyright 1996 by Beacon Hill Press of Kansas City. Available from the publisher.

Finally, we acknowledge the students, our future colleagues in ministry. They have influenced this work, not to mention our lives, beyond measure. May this book aid in the dialogue as we seek to model our lives after our Lord and Savior Jesus Christ, to whom all ultimate acknowledgement is due.

David Whitelaw
Editor

FOREWORD

The traditional understanding of a divine call to ministry appears to be undergoing change. In former days the "call" was generally viewed as "a call to preach." Happily, I can report that today's college students continue to witness to a divine call; seldom, however, is it a call to preach. Most often it is a more generic call to ministry or service. In following this call, some may eventually be led to a preaching ministry such as pastoring. Most will probably be involved in more non-conventional ministry forms throughout their professional lives. How are we to interpret this apparent departure from the former pattern?

That massive cultural changes are dramatically influencing the church is obvious. That God would inspire a new ministry paradigm to accommodate the changes within society should not be a surprise. We can either resist the changing patterns and try to hold on to the old models, or we can anticipate that the creative God just might have a new strategy for ministry today.

Obviously the church will always need preachers. Paul made this very clear: ". . . 'Everyone who calls on the name of the Lord will be saved.' How, then, can they call on the one they have not believed in? And how can they believe in the one of whom they have not heard? And how can they hear without someone preaching to them" (Rom. 10:13, 14 NIV)? We need preachers! We must keep this challenge before our youth. We must find some innovative ways to encourage people to be open to this biblically-based and time-honored ministry. May God increase among us the numbers of those who exclaim with deep conviction, "For necessity is laid upon me. Woe to me if I do not preach the gospel" (I Cor. 9:16 RSV)!

Additionally, we must acknowledge that God may again be doing a "new thing" (Isa. 43:19 NIV). This may require a new understanding among us regarding "the call" and "the ministry." This book is an initial attempt to interpret what constitutes ministry now and what form it may take in the new millennium. The college campus is the appropriate venue for dialogue on this subject. I commend the people of our Department of Philosophy and Religion who are thinking biblically, theologically, and practically about these matters so vital to the church. This book should provide some maps and models for ministry in these changing times.

Jim Bond, President
Point Loma Nazarene College

PREFACE

With any new societal territory comes the need for a new compass,
new cartographers, expansive new maps. For Fugard, writing is
his compass, his way of making sense of history and making
. . . place . . . [for the] future.
Michael Phillips on Athol Fugard, South African Playwright

The twenty-first century poses a vast horizon of new opportunities and challenges for Christian leaders. Ministers who bear the light of the Gospel face a myriad of conflicting church expectations and cultural pressures. Are we called to be therapists who help people feel better, or prophets calling society to repentance and radical conversion? Are we called to be theologians or practitioners, liberals or conservatives? While charting our ecclesiastical, social and political mission, a lingering question remains: "What does God want us to be?" This book attempts to help aspiring ministers answer this question. It is meant to be a map for those embarking on a journey of a lifetime service to God.

The contributing authors recognize that ministry is not limited to the work of professionally-trained pastors. Ministry is the work of *all* the people of God—the ordained clergy and the laity. It includes worship (*leitourgia*), witness (*marturia*), proclamation (*kerygma*), and service (*diakonia*).

The writers also recognize that within the church, some are called to specialized roles of ministry. They serve and equip the whole body of

Christ to do God's work. Thus, ministry is never a solo adventure. Ministers produce fruit for the Kingdom only as they are connected with God (Part One), with others in God's community, the church (Part Two), and with God's world (Part Three).

Maps and Models for Ministry is the work of ten full-time professors and seven actively engaged pastoral leaders. Each has spoken from a particular area of experience—"practical thinkers and thinking practitioners." Without claiming to know with certainty what ministry in the twenty-first century might be, they share a growing conviction that serious leaders not only are called to cherish the best of their own tradition but also to seek transformation for the future.

Throughout, ministers-in-the-making who enroll in Introduction to Ministry classes have been considered. These students will want to become serious scholars and learners. They are captive to a culture that constantly changes and demands that they become primarily good managers and entrepreneurs as well as healers of human pain. To embody the tough compassion of Jesus the servant is no light challenge. Let the journey to lifelong learning and ministry begin.

David Whitelaw and Janine Metcalf

PART ONE

GOD CONNECTING WITH ME FOR MINISTRY

*T*he starting point of the ministerial journey is not our personal initiative but the call of God. Our response to that call is dramatically shaped by our perception of God, revealed in the incarnate Word, Christ, and the written Word, the Bible. This section explores the theological movements that have influenced our present view of God. The focus then moves to the nature of God's call and the tools necessary to faithfully embark on a lifetime of Christlike service.

CHAPTER ONE

A TIME FOR NEW BEGINNINGS

Herb Prince

The Hebrew Bible begins with the words, "In the beginning God created the heavens and the earth" (Gen. 1:1 RSV). The first key word is
not "God," as one might expect, but "beginning." God has no beginning.
The first word is implicitly about creation, the world.[1] With the opening
word of beginning, of what God has created, the world takes on importance. God looks on what has been created *de novo* and calls it "good." By
faith, Christians believe in *creatio ex nihilo*,[2] that God created the world out
of nothing.[3] The world is created not out of God's own Being (pantheism),
created not so the divine can step away in hermitic detachment (deism),
but created, yes, so God can be involved in the world's history (theism). If
Walter Brueggemann is right, the Genesis account is a bold new intellectual tradition in which human issues are reduced to one fundamental perspective: the relationship between the Creator and the world (12).

The assigned topic is to treat God and the world, preferably in 25 words
or less! When I first came to college as an undergraduate, I could have fulfilled the assignment in less than 25 words. God was the reason for being
on campus. The world was largely a matter of indifference since little
direct attention was given to creation other than to enjoy nature's beauty.
A surprising thing happened through the college years; my perception
changed. It began to dawn on me that life is holistic. The study of philosophy opened new vistas, with other disciplines re-affirming the change. Life
experiences impacted as well. For some, God was not so obvious. A termi-
nal illness can be a "drag" on belief in God. A child dying of inoperable
cancer can make a person question if there is a God and, if God exists, is
God "good"? For others, confidence in salvation faded with their youth,
and some dropped out of school before the senior year. There were even a
few who refused to commit themselves beyond themselves, how else to
later explain Sheilaism! This is a young nurse's name for her own form of
faith. As Sheila says: "I believe in God. I'm not a religious fanatic. I can't
remember the last time I went to church. My faith has carried me a long
way. It's Sheilaism. Just my own little voice" (Bellah 221).

In what follows a schematic is outlined of the role that the God/world relation has exercised in the last two centuries. The relationship has been at the heart of theological reflection, influencing how Christians have looked upon God, the world and Christian ministry. Is ministry just to save souls, or does Christian ministry include broader, corporeal elements as well? Is ministry primarily for the ordained clergy, or does ministry apply to the laity also? Such questions have driven pastors, educators, and ecclesiastical figures to ponder long and deeply on the identity of Christian ministry with respect to purpose, education, training, and practice. Part I briefly discusses the importance of God and the world. Part II offers a succinct overview of recent Protestant thinking, noting the focus earlier in the twentieth century on God's transcendence and the shift underway since the 1960s to God's immanence. Part III concludes by highlighting issues, persons and movements affecting Christian thinking, practice and ministry as the century concludes. Running through the three parts of my essay is a singular motif: God takes the world seriously, for the world is the locus of ministry.

I

This writer believes, with John Cobb, that "against those who see us as being forced to choose God *or* the world, I am affirming that we must choose God *and* the world" (*World* 9). Indirectly, the present chapter centers around the conjunction "and." Compared to God, the world in association with the divine makes for an "odd couple." It is obvious, to the Christian, that God must be considered. God is *a se*, as the theologians put it.[4] Affirmations of God's eternality confound human understanding and become assumptions (for philosophers) or convictions (for theologians). God is the Creator of heaven and earth, of things seen and unseen as the ancient creeds affirm. "By faith we understand that the worlds were prepared by the word of God, so that what is seen was made from things that are not visible" (Heb.11:3). By God's power and wisdom, God's eternal providential care stands behind human history. The world, on the other hand, is finite, limited, temporal, and dependent. It may not be as obvious that the world, too, counts. There is a "tradition" of thinking that teaches that the world is insignificant. Known as Gnosticism (from the Greek, *gnosis*, for knowledge), this position finds matter inherently evil, believes that Jesus did not really have a human body, that Jesus did not really die but only appeared to do so on the cross, that the entire Old Testament can be discarded, and so forth. Gnosticism is a strong temptation for Christians. However, rejection of Gnosticism began almost immediately in the first century, as shown in the Johannine literature, and has continued down to the present.[5] If Gnosticism is true, Christian affirmations on creation, the

14

incarnation of Jesus, and redemption are all suspect. If Gnosticism is accepted, the world ceases to be a place of God's interest.

Historic Christianity has continually affirmed the necessity of an "and," for Christian wisdom decided long ago that God and the creation stand together. This stand is not a symmetrical relationship of equals. If symmetrical, then the relationship of God to the world would be the same as the relation of the world to God. There would be codependency. God would "need" the world just as the world would "need" God. Christianity said "No!" placing its faith in an asymmetrical understanding. God is the Creator and the world is clearly dependent for its existence upon its Maker.[6] The relationship of God to the world is not the relationship of the world to God.[7] God is God, the creation is clearly secondary. But being second is no small matter since the world is God's creation. Thus Rob Staples can call the cosmos a "sacramental universe."[8]

God and the world form a background for the minister-to-be's foreground, for each person assumes a stance on God and the world when reflecting upon life's important issues. Who am I? Who is God? How is the divine known? What is God doing in the world? Why is there something, rather than nothing? One's personal identity is a case in point. Who you are is worked out in conjunction with an "other." A major portion of each person's life is lived with whatever or whoever is in relation (an "other") with that person. In some points of view, one is constituted by relations. Developments in biology, anthropology, social psychology, and sociology argue for seeing the human being as an integral being. Human beings are not isolated "souls." To artificially separate the body and soul, fact and value, objectivity and subjectivity, nature and history, God and the world, and creation and redemption seem to reflect by-gone eras more than current findings would suggest. While not entirely determined by historical events and influences, the end of the twentieth century is decidedly different than it was at the beginning. Implications for Christian ministry seem to follow the trend. An examination of historical developments are in order, accounting for what is presently being done and urged to be done.[9]

II

An overview of recent Protestant thinking notes the historical background in thought that focused on God's transcendence earlier in this century and the shift to world and God's immanence currently underway. That a shift has occurred is common knowledge among theologians, the two periods (1920-'60 and 1960-'90) are vastly different. Ushered in during the 1920s by a then unknown pastor, Karl Barth, the resulting focus on the transcendence of God created and nurtured a generation of Christian readers. Themes such as the sovereignty of God, the sinfulness of human existence, the authority of the Bible, the centrality of the Christ-event, all

15

provided motifs that many came to take for granted. Reacting against nineteenth century liberal theology,[10] Barth (and others) claimed to show so-called "modern man"[11] what he was really like—a creature who had grown into a lover of the world. Barth has since passed to his reward (d. 1968). So have his "colleagues": Paul Tillich, Rudolf Bultmann, Friedrich Gogarten, and Emil Brunner, to name a few. The impact of their work insofar as it reflects a theological tradition (generally called Neoorthodoxy in the United States)[12] remains in a few quarters, providing a background for the emergence of a number of different points of view today. What accounts for the interests in divine transcendence earlier and divine immanence presently? Who were the prominent figures and what were the issues that have brought Protestant thought to the present? The place to begin is with the modern "turn to the subject."

The "turn to the subject" is a focus on the centrality of the individual. In technical terms, this is called nominalism—the belief that only individuals exist. In the sixteenth century nominalism became known as "the modern way," indicating a turn away from medieval thought and its concern for "universals." The focus on the individual leads through two histories: one religious, leading into Luther and the Protestant Reformation; the other through modern philosophy. Thus, the focus on the individual in the twentieth century has a philosophical root in seventeenth-century continental rationalism, more specifically in Rene Descartes. Shut up alone in a narrow enclosure he discovered the one thing he could not doubt was that he was doubting. He subsequently formulated his discovery as *cogito ergo sum* (I think therefore I am). Descartes was a Christian and an idealist. Self-knowledge and knowledge of God provided support for the belief in an extended world.

The revolutionary theme in Descartes' formula is the prominence given to the "I," the self. Because of the existence of the I, one can then posit God and finally the world. The order is significant: the individual becomes the subject. In the order of knowing, the human soul is the foundation of truth and certitude, with God and the world following. No longer does the cosmos necessarily provide the context (as for the Greeks), nor does God (as medieval Christians thought), but now it is the solitary I, the ego, the soul. This becomes one of the hallmarks of modern thinking—the ascendancy of the solitary I. To be sure, Descartes does not draw the full implications his discovery suggests. He is a citizen of his time and place, a century marked by metaphysical creativity, personal certainty and rational confidence. However, since Descartes, western thought can be largely summarized as the slow but increasing realization of the implications resident in the *cogito*.

By the nineteenth century the implications were drawn. With the skepticism of the Enlightenment in the background, Christendom's authority and the reality of God were undercut through the rise of historical consciousness. Interpreters as Ludwig Feuerbach and Friedrich Nietzsche saw no need for the divine. For Feuerbach, theological statements are really anthropological statements. To speak of the power of God is taken as a statement about the power of human existence. For Nietzsche, a God would only impinge upon human freedom. Thus Nietzsche writes of the man who runs out into the marketplace crying: "Whither is God? . . . I shall tell you. We have killed him—you and I. All of us are his murderers . . . God is Dead. . . . There has never been a greater deed" (95-96)! God becomes a mere projection on the cosmic screen. Objective grounds upon which to posit certainty no longer are said to exist. It is by one's personal decision that meaning is found in life; the focus does not come from without.

It was left to Friedrich Schleiermacher and others in the nineteenth century to make the case for a God in the midst of the "cultured despisers" of religion. This occurred by making the world the locus of God's activity. For Schleiermacher, knowledge of God came from some ultimate "whence," a whence that occurred when encountering the world. Where is God found? God is said to be found in the world. Other aspects of thought then fall in line behind this claim, making for a new appreciation of the world in the Romantic Movement. The sinfulness of human existence is minimized. Modern science reinforces attention on the world later in the century with persons as Charles Darwin making a succession of claims, and thus lifting the natural sciences to a place of prominence. Based on a principle of continuity in nature, it was not difficult for liberal theology to see progress at work in the world.

For Karl Barth, 1914 was a decisive year. The outbreak of World War I was empirical evidence that something was wrong with nineteenth-century liberalism.[13] World wars should not occur when the world is getting better! For Barth, the Bible provided a new interpretative grid. In opposition to an immanent God, Barth focused on the transcendence of God. God as the "Wholly Other" was thought to provide a basis for authority, thereby stemming the tide of relativism. As Barth put the matter: God is in heaven and human beings are on earth. There is an "'infinite qualitative distinction' between time and eternity" (*Epistle* 10). Barth's starting point was "*Dominus dixit*'—the Lord has spoken" (Zahrnt 19)! Above all, God has been revealed in the person of Jesus Christ. Natural theology and its optimistic rendering of human ability receive a definitive *Nein*. Barth later admitted he overreacted, but he still held firm to his convictions. So much stress was placed on redemption, on deliverance from sin, that the world lost some of its rightful importance. Protestant neoorthodox theology "attempted to build a wall between theology and science," focusing almost exclusively on faith and history (Yandall 459). It was left to others to attempt some measure of balance. This occurred in the 1960s.

17

III

Recent developments in American culture, theological thought and Christian ministry have one thing in common, the belief that God is at work in the world. "World" now means not only the physical world or nature but the cultural, social, economic and political dimensions in which God is said to be operative. "The philosophers [and theologians] have only *interpreted* the world in various ways; the point is to *change* it."[14] The 1960s became an era of involvement; social activism became widespread, even in "doing theology." The Vietnam War, the peace movement ("make love, not war"), the rise of Black, Third World and feminist liberation movements, Civil Rights marches, concern for the environment, and the Second Vatican Council, are but a few of the major developments during the decade. For Harvey Cox, in his best-selling volume, *The Secular City* (1965), expanding communications and interstate highways were evidence of "a world come of age." Cox was not alone. Confidence and optimism reigned. Attempts were made to overcome all forms of modern dualism, of mind and body, of religion and science, of theology and philosophy, of fact and value, of creation and redemption, of *geschichte* and *historie*.

Process theology, as an example, shows the 1960s response at work. Cosmology was put back on the discussion table due to advances in physics and the biological sciences. Older static notions of unchanging substance were replaced with the categories of process, of development and of change. Followers of Alfred North Whitehead and Pierre Teilhard de Chardin argued that substantial modifications in Christian thinking were needed. As John Cobb observed, modern nihilism was brought about by the collapse of cosmological supports (*Christian* 15). A Christian natural theology was proposed as a corrective. The charge was simple: Protestant theology earlier in the century refused to see the stage (nature) participating in the drama (history). Barth and those in his train were criticized for refusing to see creation participating in redemption.

With the exception of Evangelicals and Fundamentalists, what followed was a line of contemporaries who either stressed or tended to favor an emphasis on the Holy Spirit's relation to the natural world. This was a new song in mainline Protestant theology. Of particular interest was the attention given to creation but now in the context of the Third Person (the Holy Spirit) and not primarily the First Person (God the Father). This turn to a creation stance, with attention given to the natural sciences and the physical world, was reflected in the work of Wolfhart Pannenberg, Jurgen Moltmann, John Cobb, and Sallie McFague, to cite a few. Unlike traditional Protestant theology with its tendency to limit the scope of the Spirit's work to the heart of the believer,[15] the work of God was re-evaluated, suggesting for the future a theology of earth.

Where Barth favored transcendence and a focus on God's distance from the world, feminist theologians emerged to stress God's immanence, God at work in human experience. For Rosemary Radford Ruether, feminist theology is distinguished by "its use of *women's* experience, which has been almost entirely shut out of theological reflection in the past" (13). A re-thinking of historic Christianity comes into play. Patriarchal elements in the Christian Church must be overcome. Can one respond to God-talk such as "God the Father" if one's own father is abusive? Can a "male savior" be good news for a woman who feels powerless? Metaphors compatible with God as friend, companion, lover and even mother began to figure prominently in Christian discourse. Related issues also became part of the agenda: women in ministry, ordination, socio-economic implications for home, profession, and position, worship resources with inclusive language, and bioethics. Traditional appeals to the separation of body and soul gave way to calls for "connections," for "synergy," for holistic unity in which the human body is valued as the creation of God irrespective of the body's age.

Actions of black Christians and Third World Latin Americans insured public attention on social and economic conditions, with the militant aspect of these movements slowly giving way to more moderate, traditional values as social conditions improved. Out of these liberation efforts, an appreciation emerged for the interdependency of actual practice with theoretical substance. "Praxis" became a part of the theological vocabulary. The oppression experienced by people of color was not only seen but also personally experienced by many. Some even lost their lives in efforts to change conditions. Time was no longer simply chronology (*chronos*); time had become *kairos*.

Evangelicals and Fundamentalists have had limited success in establishing influence in the world of ideas. What they have been able to do is provide connections to historic Christianity and to give a measure of perspective to discussions. On a broad scale, they too show renewed interest in the immanence of God. The strong identification with family issues, a variety of social concerns and political interests are all indicators of closer attention to the world. Wesleyans also have had modest success. The return to church origins since the 1960s, as evidenced in the rediscovery of the Wesleyan-Holiness tradition in American life, has served Christianity in general and the Church of the Nazarene in particular. "John Wesley as a theologian" has stimulated numerous scholarly studies, including a critical edition of his works. Implications of the older Wesley's thought on creation are being mined for possible resources. Significant persons in the American Holiness Movement are being looked at seriously. Development of a Wesleyan perspective is perhaps receiving its first sustained examination in terms of psychology. Service to the poor and a renewed focus on women in ministry are bringing new hope and vitality into the movement.

Complicating matters is "the challenge of postmodernism."[16] In the 1990s, some voices are arguing that the 1960s "revolt" was still under the influence of "modern" thinking, that the modern way with its Enlightenment themes of rationality and individuality are obsolete for the twenty-first century. How this cry for the postmodern will ultimately influence history remains to be seen. The present is always difficult to judge historically. What is evident is that ministry always occurs in the present, so the postmodern (however it be defined) must be considered by those contemplating ministry.

Given the above figures, issues and movements, it is not surprising that fresh efforts are at work to define ministry for clergy and laity. The 1990s are a time of new beginnings. Today, creation ("world") can no longer be divorced from redemption ("salvation"). Concern rests with the creative effort to make theory ("theological understanding of God and world") and practice ("Christian ministry") whole. To even write of theory *and* practice is to perpetuate the separation! Perhaps the interdependency will best be lived out in terms of orthopraxis, of right practice. This may require new maps and models of ministry. The intent of the following chapters is to help the creative process along.

NOTES

1. A helpful discussion on the various uses of "world" in Scripture is given by Hermann Sasse, *Theological Dictionary of the New Testament*, trans. Geoffrey W. Bromiley, ed. Gerhard Kittel, 10 vols. (Grand Rapids, MI: Eerdmans, 1965) 3: 868-895.

2. The full formula attributed to Augustine is: "*Creatio ex nihilo, non de Deo, sed ex nihilo* (creation out of nothing, not out of God, but out of nothing)," as reported by H. Ray Dunning, 244.

3. Helpful handbooks dealing with theological concepts and terms include Van Harvey, *A Handbook of Theological Terms* (New York: Macmillan, 1964) and Donald W. Musser and Joseph L. Price, eds., *A New Handbook of Christian Theology* (Nashville: Abingdon P, 1992).

4. *Aseity* refers to God's "underived existence." As Otto Weber notes, "the *a se esse* of God was first emphatically stressed by Anselm [d. 1209] and has been a standing element in dogmatics ever since" (417).

5. For a historical overview, see Ioan P. Culianu, *The Tree of Gnosis: Gnostic Mythology from Early Christianity to Modern Nihilism*, trans. H.S. Wiesner and Ioan P. Culianu (San Francisco: Harper, 1992).

6. Among many scriptural examples, see Ps. 104, Rom. 1, Col. 1:15-17; for historical instances see esp. Augustine and the Reformed (Calvinistic) tradition where the difference between God and the world has perhaps had its strongest advocates, thereby preserving the often quoted citation: *soli Deo Gloria*. See the helpful summary by Alister E. McGrath, *Christian Theology: An Introduction* (Oxford: Blackwell, 1994) 234.

7. In the twentieth century, process theology is noted for its qualification of the traditional understanding by making dependency work both ways. Just as the world is dependent upon God, so God is dependent on the world. As a form of philosophical theology, the intent in part is to provide a uniform scheme of ideas for understanding God and the world. See esp. Alfred N. Whitehead, *Process and Reality*.

8. The sacramental universe notion is used to affirm a continuity of nature and grace, making relations between creation and redemption possible. This teaching reinforces the importance of sacraments and prevenient grace. See Rob Staples, *Outward Sign and Inward Grace*, 82-84.

9. For a detailed overview of nineteenth and twentieth-century theological developments, see Stanley J. Grenz and Roger E. Olson, *20th Century Theology: God and the World in a Transitional Age* (Downers Grove, IL: Zondervan, 1992).

10. Liberal theology is used here in its technical theological sense. The term refers to nineteenth-century Protestant thought which wedded the results of the Enlightenment to Christian thought and practice. Liberal theology (sometimes called Cultural Protestantism) shared assumptions and a pattern of thinking compatible with modern scientific developments. This thinking begins with Friedrich Schleiermacher and concludes around 1914 with the beginning of World War I. A critical overview is provided by Karl Barth, *Protestant Theology in the Nineteenth Century: Its Background and History*, trans. Brian Cozens and John Bowden (London: SCM P, 1972).

11. To write of "modern man" is to use language prominent before the 1960s. For example, "modern man" is used frequently by Rudolf Bultmann in his influential 1941 essay, "New Testament and Mythology," *Kerygma and Myth*, trans. Reginald H. Fuller, ed. Hans Werner Bartsch (New York: Harper, 1961) 1-44. The concern and then the move to inclusive, gender-free language is itself a shift that began in the 1960s with the rise of feminist theology. In the present chapter, gender usage in quotations and references remains consistent with the publication and/or time period in which the work appeared.

12. For an overview of Neoorthodox positions, see William Hordern, *The Case for A New Reformation Theology* (Philadelphia: Westminster P, 1959). For a readable account of Barth, Bultmann, Tillich and others, see Hordern's *A Layman's Guide to Protestant Theology* (New York: Macmillan, 1955).

13. Barth writes of the horror of reading in 1914 the support given by 93 German intellectuals to the war policy of Kaiser Wilhelm I, including most of his theological teachers. On that day, he writes, "For me, 19th century theology no longer held any future," in "Evangelical Theology in the 19th Century," *The Humanity of God,* trans. Thomas Wieser (Richmond, VA: John Knox P, 1966) 14.

14. The quotation is Marx's famous eleventh thesis on Feuerbach. See Karl Marx, "Theses on Feuerbach," 402.

15. The loss of nature in Protestantism is largely attributed to the influences of Augustine and Luther. Both are characterized as pursuing the theme of God, the soul and nothing more, in George Hendry's *Theology of Nature* (Philadelphia: Westminster P, 1980) 16-17.

16. See David S. Dockery, ed., *The Challenge of Post-Modernism: An Evangelical Engagement* (Wheaton, IL: Victor Books, 1995). In this work, the challenge of postmodernism is examined in relation to theology, hermeneutics, apologetics, Christian ministry and the future.

WORKS CITED

Barth, Karl. "Evangelical Theology in the 19th Century." *The Humanity of God.* Trans. Thomas Wieser. Richmond, VA: John Knox P, 1996.

—. *The Epistle to the Romans.* Trans. from 6th ed. by Edwyn C. Hoskyns. London: Oxford P, 1968.

Bellah, Robert N. et al. *Habits of the Heart: Individualism and Commitment in American Life.* New York: Harper, 1985.

The Bible. New Revised Standard Version.

The Bible. Revised Standard Version.

Brueggemann, Walter. *Genesis. Interpretation: A Bible Commentary for Teaching and Preaching.* Atlanta: John Knox P, 1982.

Cobb, John, Jr. *A Christian Natural Theology: Based on the Thought of Alfred North Whitehead.* Philadelphia: Westminster P, 1965.

—. *God and the World.* Philadelphia: Westminster P, 1969.

Dunning, H. Ray. *Grace, Faith and Holiness: A Wesleyan Systematic Theology.* Kansas City: Beacon Hill P, 1988.

Marx, Karl. "Theses on Feuerbach." *Writings of the Young Marx on Philosophy and Society.* Trans. Loyd D. Easton and Kurt H. Guddat. Garden City: Anchor Books, 1967.

Nietzsche, Friedrich. "The Gay Science." *The Portable Nietzsche.* Ed. and trans. Walter Kaufmann. New York: Viking P, 1968.

Ruether, Rosemary Radford. *Sexism and God-Talk: Toward a Feminist Theology.* Boston: Beacon P, 1983.

Staples, Rob. *Outward Sign and Inward Grace: The Place of Sacraments in Wesleyan Spirituality.* Kansas City: Beacon Hill P, 1991.

Weber, Otto. *Foundations of Dogmatics.* Vol.1 of 2 vols. Trans. and annotated by Darrell L. Guder. Grand Rapids, MI: Eerdmans, 1981.

Whitehead, Alfred N. *Process and Reality: An Essay in Cosmology.* Ed. and corrected by David Ray Griffin and Donald W. Sherburne. New York: Free P, 1978.

Yandall, Keith E. "Protestant Theology and Natural Science in the Twentieth Century." *God and Nature: Historical Essays on the Encounter between Christianity and Science.* Ed. David C. Lindberg and Ronald L. Numbers. Berkeley: U of California P, 1986.

Zahrnt, Heinz. *The Question of God: Protestant Theology in the Twentieth Century.* Trans. R.A. Wilson. New York: Harcourt, 1966.

Prince, Herb, *D.Div. Professor Prince teaches philosophy, theology, and church history at Point Loma Nazarene College. During his 25 years at PLNC Prince has served in several administrative capacities, chairing the Department of Philosophy and Religion, the Faculty Council and various institutional committees. His articles have appeared in denominational publications and in several theological dictionaries. He is an active layman in his local church.*

CHAPTER TWO

CALLED TO MINISTRY: SOME PATRISTIC PERSPECTIVES

Gerard Reed

Following one of his sermons, Dr. Pierce Harris, a prominent Atlanta pastor, met a young man who said, "Dr. Harris, I am thinking about taking up the profession of the ministry, and I would like to talk with you about it."

In response, Dr. Harris abruptly said: "Well, son, there is no need for us to talk. I can tell you right now. Don't do it!" Explaining his words to the surprised youth, Harris continued: "It's a very, very poor profession. In the first place, they don't pay you very much for what they expect you to do. You have to study harder than a teacher and have more enthusiasm than an insurance salesman. You have to make more speeches than a lawyer, and more house calls than a doctor. Besides all that, you have to be an administrator of an adult nursery. Take my advice. Don't do it."

Then, after letting those words soak in, Harris said: "Don't go into it as a profession, but if in the stillness of some hour, a power comes over your soul, a feeling of the eternal working within you, and you hear God asking, 'Whom will I send?' then don't let anything in the world dissuade you from answering 'Here am I. Send me.' The ministry is a poor profession, but it's a tremendous calling" (Spain 12-13).

In calling us, just as he called His "disciples" and urged them to make "disciples," our Lord Jesus Christ illustrated the *called*-ness of the Christian ministry. In calling *disciples,* Jesus also stressed the role of education (since "disciples" are "learners"), fleshing out that call in disciplined followers, those whom God draws into the high calling of proclaiming His Good News. As he said, in John 15:16, "You did not choose me but I chose you and appointed you that you should go and bear fruit, and that your fruit should remain, that whatever you ask the Father in my name He may give you" (NKJV). So St. Paul claimed he was "called to be an apostle, separated to the gospel of God" (Rom. 1:1 NKJV).

The first five centuries of church history illustrate some of the ways Christians understood what constituted a called ministry. Envision three pillars fundamental to the construction and preservation of ministry in the early Christian church. First, there were *positions*: clearly delineated ordained offices, with role expectations (if not "job descriptions") which gave those ordained to ministry a designated, acceptable way to fulfill their vocation. Second, there was a *process*: what we might call a congregational-ly-anointed, rather than an individually-appointed method of clergy selection. Third, there was a distinctly personal *preparation* to the process: gifted teachers or bishops attracted young disciples who became involved in the devotional and pastoral activities of the congregation, and were given an opportunity to develop Christian character as well as learn the techniques of day-to-day ministry.

Positions: Clerical Offices

A strata of clerical roles emerges in the New Testament—bishops, pres-byters, and deacons. Though scholars debate how early these positions became stratified, much evidence indicates that by the end of the first cen-tury, 70 years after Christ, the Early Church clearly stressed the impor-tance of such persons officially "ordained to the ministry."

The "First Letter [of Saint Clement] to the Corinthians," was written by the fourth Bishop of Rome—a man who was possibly the "fellow-worker" of Paul listed in Philippians 4:3, in the judgment of Origen and Eusebius. He was an "elder," Tertullian says, who was ordained by St. Peter. He wrote to extinguish an "abominable and unholy schism" due to laymen rebelling against their leaders, tearing apart the church in Corinth.

"The Apostles received the Gospel for us from the Lord Jesus Christ," Clement wrote, and preached "throughout the country and the cities, [and] they appointed their first-fruits, after testing them by the Spirit, to be bishops and deacons of those who should believe" (Letter 57, 42). The Corinthian rebels, he said, must "submit to the presbyters" (Letter 57, 42).

A contemporary of Clement, St. Ignatius of Antioch, was born ca. 30 AD and became the third bishop of Antioch, succeeding Evodius, who suc-ceeded St. Peter himself (according to an ancient tradition). Ignatius would die a martyr's death in Rome when Trajan was emperor. On his way to Rome he wrote some faith-filled letters wherein one finds, along with his vibrant testimony, an emphasis on the importance of ordained clergy: bishops; priests; deacons. For "apart from these there is nothing that can be called a church" (103).

To become a deacon, said St. Polycarp—who had studied under the Apostle John in Ephesus and had been ordained by him as Bishop of Smyrna—one "must be blameless in the presence of His justice, like ser-vants of God and Christ, not of men; not slanderers, not double-tongued, not money-lovers, temperate in all things, compassionate, careful, walking according to the truth of the Lord, who became the servant of all" (Letter 5, 138).

"And the presbyters also," Polycarp continued, "must be sympathetic, merciful to all, guiding back the wanderers, visiting all the sick, neglecting neither widow nor orphan nor pauper but 'always providing what is good before God and men.' They must refrain from all anger, from respect of persons, from unfair judgment, and keep far from all love of money; be not quick to believe anything against any man, not hasty in judgment, knowing that we are all under the debt of sin" (Letter 6, 138).

In general, deacons, presbyters, and bishops tended to be elected by congregations. By virtue of their lives, their character, and their holiness, they were elevated (often at the suggestion of other clergy) to the positions deemed appropriate for them. They were selected—and this is important, I think—because of the degree of their *sanctity*, not because they volunteered or fulfilled formal educational requirements. Sensing a call to serve, they offered themselves to the church rather than informing the church of their personally-revealed call.

The Process: Congregationally-Called

The Early Church selected its leaders less from those who professed themselves called to lead as from those whose lives and gifts seemed appropriate to certain offices. It was, of course, granted, as St. Paul said, that "If a man desires the position of a bishop, he desires a good work" (I Tim. 3:1 NKJV). Those who entered the Christian ministry sensed the Lord's call to serve. Still more: there were recognized "gifts" of the Spirit—prophecy, helps, teaching—which distinguished persons who played important roles in the body.

But the "clergy," those clearly recognized as entitled to lead or authoritatively teach, were "called" by the Lord through the Church. In Acts we read that while the believers in Antioch "were worshipping the Lord and fasting, the Holy Spirit said, 'Set apart for me Barnabas and Saul for the work to which I have called them.' So after they had fasted and prayed, they placed their hands on them and sent them off" (13:2-3 NIV).

Rather than individuals feeling personally "called" to ministry and then expecting the Church to grant them positions, leaders in the Early Church were elevated to positions because their sanctity and personality (in the judgment of discerning congregations) qualified them. One was fundamentally "called" to the religious life, "called" to a life of prayer, fasting, study, service. The basic "call" was the call to live out the Christ-life, a life of sanctity and service. If, in following that calling, one was elevated by the Church to a position of responsibility, one obeyed and then received on-the-job training. St. Ambrose, for example, received a liberal arts education and embarked upon a career as a lawyer. He entered public service and became consul of two Roman provinces. In the course of his duties, he intervened to resolve a congregational dispute in Milan, and while talking to the people a child's voice unexpectedly cried out "Ambrose Bishop." The people took this as the voice of God, so Ambrose was in rapid succession baptized, ordained to the priesthood, and consecrated bishop—all in eight days.

Now admittedly few others moved from layman to bishop in Ambrose's pattern, but the general pattern was often repeated: a church, through both its lay and clerical leaders, tended to select and ordain its clergy, men who initially preferred other vocations, especially the contemplative life. Yet when the Church called upon them, they accepted the burden of ministry.

Consider a second example: St. Augustine. Following his conversion under the influence of St. Ambrose in Milan, Augustine returned to his native land, North Africa. Here he sought to live a monastic life of prayer and study, surrounded by a few friends seeking to share his spiritual journey. Quickly his reputation grew, so that when Bishop Valerius of Hippo, needing a presbyter, told his congregation that Augustine was visiting, the crowd seized him and Valerius ordained him on the spot.

Subsequently, Augustine served the church in Hippo, preaching under the direction of Valerius. (As a Greek, Valerius appreciated Augustine's eloquence in the Latin language). Then, fearing that some other church needing a bishop might elect Augustine, Valerius by-passed custom and named Augustine his "coadjutor" designated to succeed him. So Augustine reluctantly became a priest and a bishop. He would have preferred a quiet, contemplative life of prayer, study, and writing. But others saw him as a man qualified to serve, and he was virtually dragged into positions of leadership and authority.

Certainly Ambrose and Augustine were unusually gifted persons, exceptional individuals, and their clerical careers, in response to the people's demands, were unusual as well. But they were not "exceptions to the rule." They illustrate a basic truth evident in the careers of many: leadership positions and teaching responsibilities were *given by the congregations and bishops*, not prepared for and sought by individuals.

Personalized Preparation

Clergy did not so much "go to school" as gather around a gifted pastor. To a degree, this was typical of the ancient world where one obtained an education by associating with a certain teacher and learning until one could do the same. The relationship between younger and older clergy (deacons and bishops, for example) tended to be almost familial. Numbers of young men collected around and helped in the ministerial efforts of distinguished pastors.

Before they were ordained, they took part in the life and ministry of the congregation. Prior to baptism (or confirmation) they went through a course of study, and thereafter those who were drawn to the religious life continued their study under the guidance of the bishop and clergy. Clergy did not study to secure a specific appointment; rather they studied while involved in ministry. When ordained to a position they specialized their studies in appropriate ways.

In time, by progressing through established "orders" (deacon, priest, bishop), leading clergy profited from a period of study and learning which involved practical service and preaching as well as theological reflection. Consider the example of St. Basil of Caesarea, one of the greatest Fathers of Eastern Orthodoxy. Born in Cappadocia, reared by a wealthy and remarkable family, Basil gained an excellent education, studying in an idyllic village on the family estate, where he was influenced by his sister, Macrina, an illustrious, saintly woman.

In time he went to school nearby in Caesarea, and on to Constantinople, studying rhetoric and philosophy. From there he went to Athens, a city still intellectually vigorous and prestigious. Here he joined St. Gregory of Nazianzus, another Cappadocian, and cemented a lasting significant friendship, both to them and the Church. Five years of study in Athens enabled Basil to return to Caesarea the beneficiary of the finest education (in the liberal arts) then available. Thoroughly exposed to Greek literature and philosophy, equipped with a rhetorician's skill, he entered into and absorbed the intellectual milieu of his age. Returning home, he taught rhetoric, apparently intending to follow his father's exemplary political career.

Soon, however, he renounced the world and its wealth and embraced the ascetic life, which would permit pure philosophical and contemplative pursuits. Drawn to monasticism, he sold his possessions, distributed the proceeds to the poor, and established a monastery in Pontus. Together with his friend, Gregory, Basil devoured Origen's works and collected excerpts from them into a compendium entitled *Philocalis*.

Like Ambrose and Augustine, Basil was basically pushed into the priesthood, ultimately becoming Bishop of Caesarea, where he finished life in active and fruitful ministry. And part of that ministry was the training and ordaining of young clerics—men such as his brother, St. Gregory of Nyssa—who were drawn to him.

A company of young men similarly assembled around Augustine in Hippo. They lived a monastic life and learned from the teaching and example of the master. Over the years, a number of qualified clergy went out from Hippo to assume leading roles in the North African church. Through personal contact with Augustine, listening to him preach and observing him at prayer, joining together in the disciplines of study and devotion and service, the clergy received their training. His precept, "For you I am bishop; with you I am Christian," illustrated for them the model of Christian ministry.

Amazingly, these centuries witnessed a prodigious outpouring of thoughtful theology. Preachers like Ambrose became first-rate theologians while in the active ministry. Contemplatives, like Gregory of Nyssa, in the midst of their assignments, found ample time for prayer and thought and the writing of theological masterpieces. The life of the Church, for both laity and clergy, seemed to stimulate theological inquiry and insight. And, of course, the Church effectively evangelized much of the world. To understand the nature of ministerial calling and preparation, these early centuries provide models worth following.

WORKS CITED

The Bible. New International Version.

The Bible. New King James Version.

St. Clement of Rome. "First Letter to the Corinthians." Trans. Francis X. Glimm. *The Apostolic Fathers.* Washington: Catholic U of America P, 1962.

St. Ignatius of Antioch. "Letter to the Trallians." Trans. Gerald R. Walsh. *The Apostolic Fathers.* Washington: Catholic U of America P, 1962.

St. Polycarp. "Letter to the Philippians." Trans. Francis X. Glimm. *The Apostolic Fathers.* Washington: Catholic U of America P, 1962.

Spain, Robert H. *Getting Ready to Preach.* Nashville: Abingdon P, 1995.

SUGGESTED READING

St. Ambrose. *Seven Exegetical Works.* Trans. Michael P. McHugh. Washington: Catholic U of America P, 1972.

St. Augustine. *The Confessions of St. Augustine.* Trans. F. J. Sheed. New York: Sheed & Ward, 1942.

——. *Sermons on the Liturgical Seasons.* Trans. Sister Mary Sarah Muldowney. New York: Fathers of the Church, Inc., 1959.

Chadwick, Henry. *The Early Church.* London: Penguin, 1967.

Chrysostom, John. *The Works of St. Chrysostom.* Vol. 10 of The Post-Nicene Fathers. 38 vols. Grand Rapids, MI: Eerdmans, 1975.

Dudden, F.H. *The Life and Times of St. Ambrose.* 2 vols. New York: Oxford UP, 1935.

Fant, Clyde E., and Pinson, William M., eds. *Twenty Centuries of Great Preaching.* 13 vols. Waco, TX: Word , 1971.

Reed, Gerard, *Ph.D. Dr. Reed serves as College Chaplain and Professor of Bible, theology and ethics at Point Loma Nazarene College. Aside from preaching and teaching at the college, he speaks at numerous retreats and theological conferences throughout the United States. Reed is an ordained elder in the Church of the Nazarene and has served in various pastoral capacities. An avid reader, he has written more than 40 book reviews as well as a vast array of published articles on such topics as Christian ethics, church history, and preaching.*

CHAPTER THREE

GOD'S CALL AND HUMAN RESPONSE: A BIBLICAL PERSPECTIVE

Robert Smith

Is it possible for men and women to hear God's voice in the roar of the world in which we live? Can we know with certainty that God has called us to ministry at the turn of the twenty-first century? How do we identify God's voice from all the other voices in our culture? Questions like these are not easy to answer. As we examine biblical accounts of God's encounter with individuals, perhaps we can identify a pattern that will provide answers to these questions.

The Bible reveals that throughout history God has chosen to work through individuals who submit themselves to a call that cannot be ignored. Abraham, Moses, Gideon, and Jeremiah shared a common awareness of God's voice compelling them to tackle situations that seemed beyond their abilities. God's "call" caused them to alter their lives and to take on an identity they would never have chosen for themselves. As people who have been influenced by the religious expectations of late twentieth-century culture, we assume that we will be able to judge the success or failure of our ministry by our dominant cultural values. If this is so, then the stories of those great men and women of history who were obedient to God's call lived far below their expectations. What would we think of Isaiah? Would we accept God's call to ministry knowing in advance that people would not respond favorably to us? In Isaiah 6:10 God tells the prophet that his preaching will fall on deaf ears. Regardless of his preaching, people will ignore God's Word and live as they please. Would we accept the misunderstanding of Jeremiah or the indignity of Ezekiel? How could we tolerate the failure of our ministry to meet or exceed contemporary cultural expectations?

When our motive for ministry is *ambition* and our coveted goal is *success*, how do we justify God's call when circumstances shroud our ministry in despair? Early this century, John Henry Jowett discussed the *vertical* dimension of ministry. According to Jowett, this spatial metaphor states that when a person "selects the Christian ministry as his (*sic*) vocation he must have the assurance that the selection has been imperatively constrained by the eternal God" (12). Ministry is not a vocation that we choose; it is being chosen, chosen by God for a work that God creates and sustains by divine assistance. From a human point of view we are forced to ask, "Who is worthy of such a calling?" While the question is not insignificant, it is not the proper response. God's call is not grounded in the subjective experiences of men and women. Rather, it is grounded in the sovereign nature of God's character. The theological pattern of God's call is disclosed in John's Gospel; God the Father *sends* Jesus into the world and Jesus *chooses* and *sends* the disciples to do works of ministry.

The Apostle Paul recognized the sovereign call of God on his life when he disclosed his experience to the churches of Galatia: "But when He [God] who had set me apart, *even* from my mother's womb, and called me through His grace, was pleased to reveal His Son in me, that I might preach among the Gentiles . . ." (Gal. 1:15-16a NIV). From this brief account, we may conclude that "Paul can only have understood the change that took place as being analogous to a prophetic call (Ebeling 76). Thus Paul, as an apostle of Jesus Christ, was standing in the line of the great Hebrew prophets like Jeremiah of whom the Lord said, "Before I formed you in the womb, I knew you" (Jer. 1:5a NIV). Here the vertical dimension of the *call* is discussed as an act of God who speaks in personal terms for a specific purpose. This radical understanding of the nature of God does not insure the prophet that his ministry will achieve the transformation of the people of Israel. It did not assure Jeremiah that his preaching would prevent the destruction of Jerusalem by the Babylonian army. As God's prophet speaking God's Word, Jeremiah became the scapegoat for religious types who believed that God's Presence could be manipulated by ritual activities without regard for the demands of the Mosaic covenant. For at some point in the history of Israel, the people began to revere the Mosaic covenant as an unconditional covenant. From this perspective, their infidelity to *YHWH* had no impact on the fulfillment of the terms of the covenant i.e., Israel began to perceive the Mosaic covenant as an unilateral covenant rather than as a bi-lateral covenant. Thus, the human dimension was stripped away from the claims of the covenant.

Reflecting on the plight of Jeremiah, we may conclude that the God who called the prophet failed him. Such a conclusion assumes that God's call guarantees success. This assumption affirms a basic cultural value of this generation, but it does not necessarily reflect the teaching of Scripture. The character of God revealed in Scripture does not guarantee success, but God has promised to be *with us* in the diverse circumstances of life. Life itself teaches us that success is not the validation of God's call, even though it fulfills contemporary cultural expectations. A careful reading of Jeremiah presents a view of ministry that stands against the cultural values of our age. "The whole book as it stands is a literary-theological disclosure of the unraveling of a royal world, of the disintegration of a stable universe of public order and public confidence" (Brueggemann, *Pluck* 21). To be aware of the *vertical* dimension implicit in God's call in the midst of life itself is the validation of the call.

When the prophecy of Jeremiah is read through the lens of a *theology of the cross*, a clear analogy is observed between ministry in the Old Testament and ministry in the New Testament. When ministry is carried out from this prophetic standpoint, a biblical intention is created when we recognize that "the theology of the cross takes as its point of departure the brokenness of the human spirit and the human community. It places hope in God's transformative solidarity with fallen creation, with the world *in* its brokenness" (Hall 28). This prophetic pattern of ministry teaches us that those who are called of God continue to minister in spite of the adverse conditions within the world. They are not looking for notoriety, but they do the work of ministry to fulfill the divine call that has gripped their lives.

The Bible does not establish "how the call will come to us" (Jowett 17), nor does it set forth the time frame in which the details of the call are clarified. The Bible teaches us that God is at work in history. Time, then, is the ally of anyone considering the possibility of accepting God's call to a life of ministry. If our understanding of the call is analogous to the process of human maturity, we can conclude that the call *unfolds through time as we continue to reflect on how we may most appropriately carry out the divine seizure of our life.* While waiting for the call to be clarified, the "called" one will continue to develop a spiritual life necessary to sustain a ministry for the twenty-first century. Spiritual sensitivity is a tangible sign of God's call. Coupled with this is the delight that comes from associating with God's people, the Church. Here is the place where we find people with similar values who, through the ministry of the Holy Spirit, can affirm God's call on our life. The function of the Church, then, is to provide nurture and a place of service while the details of God's call are clarified. Thomas Oden urges the person who is contemplating the reality of God's call to "let an initial impression grow quietly in a community of prayer until it becomes a sustained conviction" (18).

The Bible does not contain a typical pattern which reveals how God calls men and women to ministry. In spite of this, a brief examination of the call of Moses points out characteristics that recur in other "call narratives." The story begins with a setting that is characterized by curiosity. The attention of Moses is captured by a bush that refuses to be consumed by fire. As his curiosity moves him to examine this strange desert event, Moses encounters the voice of God speaking from the flaming bush. This simple narrative has led Terence Fretheim to conclude that "*curiosity leads to call*" (54). He goes on to say, "[i]t is only when God sees that Moses actually moves to satisfy his curiosity that God calls to him; it is only as Moses allows himself to be drawn into the sphere of the unusual sight that communication takes place" (Fretheim 56).

While the curiosity of Moses cannot be overlooked, the key to this passage is the character of God. God's presence "transforms everything at hand, including the place and the conversation. . . . The place has been transformed by the speech and presence of God. Moses is now taken up into the sphere of that awful holiness" (Brueggemann, "Exodus" 712). What is more, "[t]he *holy* God enters into the suffering of the people and makes it his own" (Fretheim 56).

This simple biblical account provides several stimulating insights that may be helpful to those who are seeking to know if God is calling them to a life of ministry:

1. *Begin by examining the terrain.* Allow your curiosity to place you in situations that would allow you to be sensitive to the voice of God, e.g., youth and music programs in a local Church; short term mission trips; compassionate ministries; volunteer work, etc. Take time to experiment with various ministry opportunities.

2. *Discover who you are.* Recognize the presence of divine mystery. When Moses was confronted with God, he hid his face. Nevertheless, his ministry was initiated by God. Moses was more than an ordinary man among his Hebrew kin. Raised in the household of Pharaoh, his understanding of Egyptian language, literature, and cultural expectations prepared him for his encounter with the Egyptians. When God calls us he knows our past, our gifts and graces, as well as our needs. We need to be aware of our strengths and weaknesses so that we can be stretched by considering the expanding possibilities of God's work in the world. Read the call of Gideon in Judges 6:1-40. Aware of his weaknesses, he was startled when the angel of the LORD addressed him as a "mighty warrior" (v. 12). Nevertheless, he opened himself to the work of God in his life and led the children of Israel to a military victory over the Midianites.

3. *Develop a disciplined life.* Cultivate a lifestyle that is appropriate to the biblical teaching of the character of God. As you recognize God's holiness, be willing to *take off your shoes* spiritually as "an act of willing submission." Learn early and well that "[a] primary need of the minister is to move from being 'driven' to a sense of calling. Rediscovering our call will result in such a centering of self that both personal authenticity and spiritual growth will be the result. Daily self-examination against God's righteousness and the admission of personal finitude and limitations will be required" (Simmons 537). Like a well-trained Olympic athlete, give God your best effort. There is much more at stake than a gold medal.

4. *Follow God's direction.* As you contemplate your place in ministry "[d]on't do it if you can. But if you have to do it, give it your all" (Pollard 138). God knows the needs of the world and where your ministry can be most effective. When God called Moses, the children of Israel were still in bondage. God directed Moses to return to a people who had rejected his previous efforts to defend them. For the next 40 years Moses struggled to lead his people to their promised inheritance. Even though the people were rebellious, Moses continued to fulfill God's call on his life.

5. *Trust God!* With your future in the balance, learn to *trust* God implicitly. The biblical evidence does not lead us to believe that God "plays games" with those who sense God's call. The nature of our human condition places us between absolute certainty and the inability to move into the future. Trusting God and living by faith takes courage. Allow the ministry of the Holy Spirit to give you peace as you seek to find your place in ministry in response to God's call on your life.

If you sense God's call to ministry on your life and you are wondering what to do, begin by following the five insights we have taken from the story of Moses. Let me add a sixth insight: *Relax!* Live in an attitude of joy and thanksgiving as you continue to respond to God's call on your life. Experience has proven that God's call is not a moving target. Although the certainty of your response will always be grounded in faith—and therefore susceptible to misunderstanding—you will experience certainty as the call becomes an irresistible expression of your response to God's claim on your life.

WORKS CITED

Brueggemann, Walter. *To Pluck Up, To Tear Down: A Commentary on the Book of Jeremiah 1-25. International Theological Commentary.* Grand Rapids, MI: Eerdmans, 1988.

—. "The Book of Exodus." Vol.1 of *The New Interpreter's Bible.* 1 vol. to date. Nashville, TN: Abingdon P, 1994- .

Ebeling, Gerhard. *The Truth of the Gospel: An Exposition of Galatians.* Trans. David Green. Philadelphia: Fortress P, 1985.

Fretheim, Terence C. *Exodus. Interpretation: A Commentary for Preaching and Teaching.* Louisville, KY: John Knox P, 1991.

Hall, Douglas John. *Thinking the Faith: Christian Theology in a North American Context.* Minneapolis: Fortress P, 1991.

CHAPTER FOUR

TREASURE IN CLAY POTS: PAUL'S MINISTRY OF AFFLICTION

Jerry McCant

Jesus "was crucified as a weakling" (2 Cor 13:4)[1] is Paul's shocking way of stating it. Standing beyond Easter one might expect Paul to place a sublime halo or a hero's wreath on his story of Jesus' death. Instead the apostle offers only a stark statement of a shameful and abject incident. Paul cannot forget and allows no one else to forget the "scandal of the cross." Rather than deny or euphemize the scandal, Paul embraces it and makes it the heart of his theology.

Studying Paul's language of affliction takes us close to his deepest convictions. His theology of ministry is Christocentric: "For we are weak in Christ, in dealing with you, we will live with Christ by the power of God" (2 Cor. 13:4b).[2] Through this language he speaks of himself, his ministry and the God who calls him to be an apostle. It is the lens through which he sees the reality of life. Affliction is not simply one more topic in the Pauline compendium; it is the ground on which Paul does theology. Nowhere does the language of affliction have greater prominence than in the Corinthian correspondence. Jesus died in weakness and Paul ministers from his weakness. "Christ crucified" is what Paul preaches and he always preaches in the shadow of the Cross. One cannot read Paul's letters without encountering the Christ of the Cross and Paul's desire to emulate Jesus' ministry.

Defense of Apostleship

If Paul had not had problem churches, he would not have written letters or if he had, the letters would have been very different. Most of 2 Corinthians is an "ironic apology"[3] of Paul's ministry. The passage under discussion in this essay, 2 Corinthians 4:7-12, is an indisputably apologetic section of the letter. Some scholars consider it to be the central argument in chapters 1-7. While it is a defense of his ministry, this passage reveals his theology of ministry in a more general sense, not only for himself but also for everyone whom God calls to ministry.

At 1:12 Paul speaks indirectly of the problem at Corinth and defends his behavior as having been with "frankness and sincerity." He repeats this at 7:2, suggesting it is the main issue against which he offers a defense. Paul had promised to visit Corinth but broke his promise (1:15-22). His defense is that he wanted to "spare" the Corinthians another "painful visit" (1:23). He wrote a tearful letter (2:4) but the Corinthians thought it was too severe (7:8). He states the proposition for his argument: (1) In Christ I speak as a person of sincerity; (2) In Christ I speak as a person sent from God; (3) In Christ I speak as one standing in God's presence (2 Cor 2:17).

Paul is a slave in a triumphant procession (2:14) but even so he is the "aroma of Christ" (2:15). He is not "sufficient for these things" (2:16) but Christ has made him sufficient (same word as in 2:16) as "a servant of the new covenant" (3:6). This apostle is not a "peddler of God's word" (2:17), and he does not need letters of recommendation to or from the Corinthians (31-3). However, the Corinthians are his letter of recommendation (3:2). Paul compares himself with Moses and says he is a servant of a better covenant (3:7-4:1), but it is by the mercy of God that he engages in ministry. He does not proclaim himself but "Jesus Christ as Lord" and himself "as your slave for Jesus' sake" (4:5).

Treasure in a Clay Pot

After a description of the glory of the gospel that is full of assurance, Paul characterizes himself with the derogatory metaphor of a "clay pot" (4:7). There is a necessary correlation between the tribulations and frailty of the minister and the minister's compatibility as an agent of the gospel. No nimbus of glory surrounds Paul's head, but rather he emphasizes the superlative power displayed in the Lord's servant who bears a precious treasure in a clay pot. The grammar of the Greek indicates that he has the treasure in a clay pot in order to more fully display God's majestic power. God's power is on display in Paul's triumph over adversity. God is the dynamic in his ministry which Paul amplifies by denigrating himself to the status of a "clay pot."

An analysis of 4:1-6 shows the parallel with "treasure" in verse 7 and makes it clear that the "treasure" is the gospel Paul preaches. The treasure is precious but the unworthy vessel (i.e. Paul) makes a defense necessary. There is a clear grammatical connection between "this ministry" in 4:1 and "this treasure" in 4:7. To all appearances Paul is no more than a cheap earthenware clay pot. His life does not seem impressive to any keen observer. "This treasure" is not the issue in 4:7-12; at issue is how Paul, who exhibits all the frailties of human weakness, claims to be an apostle of Jesus Christ. Paul responds that a correlate of his weakness is the weakness of Christ, and the glory of his ministry is the power of God.

A clay pot connotes fragility and cheapness and is a derogatory metaphor. Although it is a "throwaway" vessel, sometimes precious treasure is stored in clay jars. In the context, Paul intends the clay pot to function as a metaphor for the body, but includes the whole person in the metaphor. The metaphor shows the contrast between human weakness and divine power. God has placed the ministry of the gospel in Paul, the clay pot, to make it evident that the power of the gospel derives from God.

At one level, Paul is boasting that "extraordinary power" characterizes his ministry. Like Seneca, Paul knows that the container makes it more difficult to recognize the treasure. Paul is proud of his work but he refuses to claim credit for his amazing success, insisting that the power at work in his ministry belongs to God, not the minister. Unlike the invincible Stoic sage, Paul is not "a man of steel." He knows too well that "power is made perfect in weakness" (2 Cor 12:9).

Unfortunately we hear only Paul's version of the Corinthian story. Apparently, the Corinthians thought Paul was not a demonstration of God's power.[4] For the Corinthians, a sick charismatic and miracle worker is oxymoronic. The Corinthians and Paul disagreed on what constitutes a demonstration of power. Paul's human weakness becomes a foil for the glorification of God with the paradoxical "treasure in a clay pot." Paul is not the powerhouse; he is only the servant through whom God displays divine power. Plato once said that "the god of set purpose sang the finest songs through the meanest of poets. . .these fine poems are not human or the work of men, but divine and the work of gods." God chose an ugly "clay pot" for the most precious treasure.

Paul interprets the weakness of his "clay pot" Christologically. Later he will write "If I must boast, I will boast of the things that show my weakness" (11:30). Again he affirms "So, I will boast all the more gladly of my weaknesses, so that the power of Christ may dwell in me. Therefore, I am content with my weakness" (12:9bc-10a). This boasting in weakness is possible because "whenever I am weak, then I am strong" (12:10d). What is more, "Christ was crucified in weakness, but lives by the power of God. For we are weak in him but. . .we will live with him by the power of God" (13:4). The catchwords "weakness" and "power" in 12:9-10 and 13:4 assure a Christological understanding of his ministry.

Paul so identifies with Christ that "the sufferings of Christ are ours" (2 Cor 1:18). In Corinth Paul's message was the foolishness of "the word of the cross" (1 Cor 1:23; 2:2) in a context of weakness. Paul carries "in the body the death of Jesus" (4:10) and this earthen vessel is "delivered over to the death of Jesus" (4:10-11). The apostle desires to be "conformed to the death of Jesus" (Phil 3:10) and he is "crucified with Christ" (Gal 2:20). Suffering and weakness belong to the schema of the apostle. He is a clay pot who boasts in his weakness. Whatever ministry Paul has, it is a cruciform ministry. He lives and works in the shadow of the cross.

There is a certain irony in Paul's description of the minister as a servant, a clay pot, bearing the precious treasure of the gospel. Inevitably Paul stands all criteria for success in the ministry on its head. Paul is not a hero (see 11:32-33) but insists he is an apostle. He returns from his ecstatic heavenly rapture with no evidence (12:1-5) but he nonetheless claims that he is an apostle. In 12:7-10, he offers a miracle story without a healing. He is no miracle worker but he is an apostle. Instead of weakness disqualifying him as a minister, it is the only qualification he has. Paul would never make it as a TV personality preaching a gospel oriented to success. It is doubtful if Paul would be at the front in the church growth movement. His only boast is his weakness and the power of God that makes use of an old clay pot.

Antithetical Suffering List

Antithesis (literally, "to set against") means opposition or resistance. In verbal or written form antithesis appeals not to logical proofs or arguments but to an emotional presentation. Quite simply the author or speaker "plays on the emotions." The persuasiveness depends on "feelings," not on rational thought processes. Aristotle thought antithesis was an ideal method to refute another opinion. He said we understand things best when we place opposites side by side. The purpose of antithesis is to infuse vehemence and passion into words. Antitheses lend credibility to one's argument, excite emotions and persuades the audience. They intensify the argument by amplifying or emphasizing and repeating the speaker's main point.

Antitheses invite the audience to become participants in the speech. You find yourself swaying along with the succession of antitheses even if you do not agree with the speaker. In cases where the audience has not reached a decision, yielding to the emotional appeal of antithesis prepares for assent to the subject identified with it. Antitheses are miniature two-sided presentations whose persuasive power is that by acknowledging counter beliefs of the audience, the speaker seems more fair and responsible in debating the issues.

With his carefully controlled ability to arrange words so they express emotion, Paul uses strong *pathos* to "prove" his case. By shifting the focus from himself to God, Paul completely transforms the imagery in his catalog of sufferings. Without the shift Paul would be like the Stoic sage who still fights on one's knees even if one falls. It is not sheer determination to rise again and fight with greater defiance that keeps Paul going. By God's power, Paul is a clay pot that, even though shattered, remains unbroken (4:9). Paul is often "knocked down" but has never been "knocked out" (4:10).

Four antithetical statements describe how Paul suffers "in every way" (4:8). He structures his tribulation list so that the contrast comes with an adversative (i.e. "but") and a negative particle (i.e. "not"). He states the thesis to which he concedes and with the words "but not," he shows the contrast with antithesis. Paul is

afflicted	but not	crushed
perplexed	but not	driven to despair
persecuted	but not	forsaken
struck down	but not	destroyed

"In every way" (4:8) and "always" (4:10) form a frame around this catalog of contrasting characteristics and amplify Paul's tribulations. Thus Paul is saying that he is always afflicted, perplexed, persecuted and struck down. This pattern persists throughout the ministry of Paul.

Two paradoxical metaphors bracket this catalog in 4:8-10: "treasure in clay pots" (4:7) and "not dying, yet carrying around the dying of Jesus" (4:9b-10a). Paul's move from 4:7 to 4:8 forms an inverted parallelism (i.e. *Chiasmus*) that looks like this:

> **A** Power belongs to God (v. 7)
> **B** Not to Paul (v. 7)
> **B'** Paul is afflicted and weak (v. 8)
> **A'** God's power keeps Paul from being crushed (v. 8)

That God tests a vessel with adversity may serve as proof that one is righteous. The Jewish Talmud teaches that God does not test the wicked but only the righteous. Paul is not an apostolic dynamo but simply a "clay pot" through whom God displays extraordinary divine power. Paul believes his sufferings validate his ministry.

Paul constructs four sets of antitheses so that in each he concedes the first item in the pair but denies the second. Surprisingly, in the first pair Paul contrasts "affliction" and "crushed." In Greek the two nouns are virtually synonymous. The first item he concedes is "affliction," the most comprehensive term in this list and the most important word for suffering in 2 Corinthians. Both terms in the first pair basically mean to press in, constrict or put under pressure. Paul is saying, "In every way (everything) I am under pressure, but because of God's power, it does not crush me." Paul has always been in "tight spots" but God has "opened" the way for deliverance (see 2 Cor 1:9-10).

Word play (i.e. pun) shapes the second antithesis. No English translation can do it justice, but it translates "despairing but not utterly desperate." Perhaps one may express the assonance by paraphrasing it to read "sometimes at a loss, but not a loser." The two words in this pair come from the same Greek word and means "to be without resources, and so to be at a loss, be in doubt or be puzzled." To give the sense of what Paul is saying we can paraphrase it "despairing but not desperate to the nth degree." Paul reports once that he was "desperate to the nth degree" (see 1:8)—he was utterly and unbearably burdened—the burden was unbearably heavy, but "the God who raises the dead" (1:9) raised Paul out of utter desperation.

In the third antithesis Paul says he is "persecuted but not forsaken." The Greek word Paul uses may be translated "persecute" or "pursue." In this passage it almost certainly has the full sense of persecute as it does in 1 Corinthians 4:12. The Greek word "forsake" or "abandon" is associated with God's promise never to forsake Israel (e.g. Gen. 28:15; Deut. 31:6, 8; Joshua 5:1; Sir. 2:10; Ps. 22:2, which Matthew [27:46] and Mark [15:34] cite). The Apostle wants to communicate to the Corinthians that God's superabounding power strips all suffering of its desperate character. God's grace removes the dread and fear of suffering and abandonment.

Finally, in the fourth antithesis Paul concedes he is always being "struck down" but declares that he is "not destroyed." J. B. Phillips has caught the sense of Paul punning word play in this antithesis with the paraphrase "knocked down but not knocked out." "Knocked down" in the Greek suggests being thrown to the ground. As it appears in this verse it might mean to be overthrown, laid low by a blow or a weapon, abused or bullied, cast down, rejected or even to be killed. "Destroy" translates a Greek word that means to destroy or kill; Paul sometimes uses this word to speak of the destruction of people who do not receive the gospel. This word is the strongest word in this antithetical catalog of suffering. It serves as a transition to Paul's remark about the "dying of Jesus" in 4:10 and the double use of death in 4:11-12. With 4:9b and 4:10a we have a paradox: He is not being killed but he always carries in his body the "dying" of Jesus.

Paradoxically Paul does not die in the persecution but he always carries about the dying of Jesus. The purpose of carrying about the "dying of Jesus" is to reveal the life of Jesus in us. Nothing could be more antithetical: the "dying of Jesus" reveals "the life of Jesus" in us. The "dying" of Jesus in Paul involves his mortification (4:12). Death is at work in him and his "outer person" is in the process of decay (see 4:16).

The putrid pungency of the "dying of Jesus" is like the "smell of death" for unbelievers (2:14) but it is the "sweet aroma of Christ" (2:15) and a "fragrance of life" (2:16) to believers. For Paul, the "dying" of Jesus in his body reveals the "life of Jesus" in his "mortal flesh" (4:11). He endures all this suffering "on account of Jesus" (4:11), thus becoming a participant in the suffering and death of Jesus. This apostle counts it a "high privilege" to suffer for Christ (Phil 1:29). He desires to know the "fellowship" of Jesus' suffering and wants to be "conformed to his death" (Phil 3:10). Suffering for and with Jesus is the trademark of ministry for Paul.

Antithesis in this Pauline catalog of suffering is quite rhythmic but not lyrical. The repeated "but not" emphasizes that although he is weak and suffers affliction, Paul has endured and survived by the power of God. Quite atypical for Paul is the repeated use of the name Jesus; it occurs six times in 4:10-14. This repetition of the name Jesus emphasizes Paul's solidarity with Jesus in his experience. Jesus is Paul's model of the Suffering Servant (see 4:5). The word "life" appears three times, twice in the phrase "the life of Jesus" (4:10-11) and once by itself (4:12). There is measured resonance and euphony in Paul's rhythmic pattern into which Paul constantly pours all the passion he can into his defense of his ministry.

Antitheses in this passage provide an arresting contrast between dreadful situations and potentially disastrous results that did not occur. Paul teases his readers into wondering why the expected consequences did not come. If he is in a tight spot, why is he not hemmed in? If he is despairing, why is he not utterly desperate? If he is persecuted, why is he not abandoned? If he is shattered on the ground, why is he not broken? Paul has a simple answer: the extraordinary power of God (4:7). Both the death and life of Jesus are present in him.

With the words "in every way" (4:8) and "always" (4:10, 11) Paul transforms a list of specific afflictions into a description of Paul's entire ministry. The paradoxical narration of suffering does not intend to convey information about Paul. It is not particular incidents of suffering that are in view. He wants to persuade them that suffering characterizes his apostolic ministry. Suffering is God's stamp of approval and validates his ministry. As one who always carries in his body "the dying of Jesus" and is "constantly being given up to death on account of Jesus" (4:10-11), Paul links his suffering with that of Jesus. He believes that Christ and his cross are the ground and cause of the suffering of every Christian.

Conclusion

Suffering and the cross of Jesus are the trademarks of Christian ministry. Without them, there is no ministry. Paul conceives of his ministry as a divine call (3:4-4:1). He believes ministry finds its validation in sincerity (4:2-6). One must conduct ministry as in the presence of God (4:13-5:10). When Paul preaches it is not as a "peddler" who waters down the Word of God (2:17). Paul does not preach himself but Jesus Christ as Lord (4:5). Paul's preaching finds its basis in his experience of believing: "I believed and so I preached" (4:13). The purpose of Paul's ministry, including his daily sufferings, is for the sake of the Corinthians and their faith. Self-aggrandizement and personal profit have no place in a Pauline view of ministry.

A minister of Jesus Christ must be a Suffering Servant. The true pastor is not a patriarch lording it over the people's faith (1:24). Ministers (literally, "slaves") must be slaves of the people they serve (4:5). A minister must be willing "to die together and live together" with the community of faith (7:3). God calls ministers to preach and God calls ministers to pastor. Paul knew how to both preach and to pastor the people. As ministers we must take the "dying" of Jesus in ourselves always. We must stay close to the Cross and beckon our parishioners to join us at the cross. There is no place for patriarchal and paternalistic attitudes that must assert authority over the flock. Paul does not allow the Corinthians to be his Patron, and he refuses to be their Patron. Only God is the patron of the people. Ministry performed in the shadow of the cross is egalitarian and equalitarian. We are all one in Christ!

God calls ministers into service and God is the source of all power for the ministry. Ministers are cheap, dispensable "clay pots" in whom God has entrusted the treasure of the gospel. We are not the gospel, only the bearer of the treasure that is of inestimable worth. Unless the power of God is at work in our ministry, we will accomplish little spiritual good. We must never succumb to "preaching ourselves," but must always proclaim Jesus Christ, the Crucified One. God calls weak, frail human beings into ministry so no one will confuse "ministerial success" with the "extraordinary power of God."

NOTES

1. This is my translation. Except when I translate for myself, all other references are to *The New Testament and Psalms: An Inclusive Version,* an adaptation of the New Revised Standard Version (New York: Oxford UP, 1995).

2. Unless otherwise indicated, all references are to 2 Corinthians; thus a briefer citation.

3. In other words, his *apologia* (defense speech) is a parody. At 12:19 Paul tells the Corinthians they have been thinking he was defending himself. However, he corrects that notion, saying he speaks "in Christ in the sight of God." He does not concede that the Corinthian community is a judicial body. Only God can judge Paul and his apostleship (I Cor. 4:3-5).

4. If there had been no disagreement on this matter, Paul probably would have never written 2 Corinthians. Although the defense is ironical and parodical, 2 Corinthians is nonetheless a defense speech. The passage here, 4:7-12 is a defense against weakness; he shows that although he is a clay pot (see the antitheses in vv. 8-9), he overcomes the weaknesses "by the extraordinary power of God" (4:7). In 4:16-5:10, he resumes the theme of defense of his weakness as an apostle. Almost everything in chapters 10-13 is a defense of

and boasting in his weaknesses. He does not wish to boast, and does so only as a fool (See 11:1ff), but comes to say "If I must boast, I will boast of the things that show my weakness" (11:30). He illustrates his weakness with parodies: (1) he never got "over the wall" but was sneaked "through the wall" (11:32-33); (2) he had an ecstatic rapture to heaven but brought back no evidence (12:1-5); (3) he must contend with a "thorn for the flesh" (i.e. "a sick Corinthian church") in the form of a healing story that has no healing (12:7-10, esp. v.9). Acceptance of God's answer that there will be no healing for the "thorn" causes Paul to say he will cease praying for healing and he will "glory or boast in his weaknesses" (12:9; also see v.5). He learns that "When I am weak, then I am strong" (12:10) and "power is made perfect in weakness" (12:9). Space limitations forbid a complete discussion of the issue. However, the evidence throughout 2 Corinthians is that the Corinthians consider him a charlatan because he claims to be an apostle but he suffers continually in his weaknesses.

***McCant, Jerry**, Ph.D. Dr. McCant is a Professor of Religion and Christian Education at Point Loma Nazarene College. During the 20 years he has served on the faculty, McCant has contributed numerous articles to theological journals and magazines. Before teaching, he pastored Nazarene churches in North Carolina, Kentucky, and Georgia.*

CHAPTER FIVE

A BIBLICALLY-SHAPED MINISTRY

Frank Carver

"He had become so Christlike, so radiant with God's love, that his entire being was ministry." (Nouwen 32) This quality of ministry, ascribed to St. Antony, a fourth century desert monk, is a ministry open to every Christian.

The Gospel of John tells us how this can be. It witnesses to the heart of a truly Christian ministry. In essence, ministry is bearing witness to Jesus Christ. As a young seminarian I knew that, and I attempted to witness in line with the models presented to me. I bought tracts at the Nazarene Publishing House and walked the streets on a Sunday afternoon. In graduate school I even attempted street preaching outside a Scottish tavern. I felt defeated however, overwhelmed by guilt, rather than empowered by grace.

In the intervening years my study of Scripture, particularly the Gospel of John, became a liberating experience. I found respite from my guilt, a new freedom and confidence, for I began to understand what being a witness means biblically. The discovery came primarily from Jesus' last words to his disciples before his crucifixion and resurrection. His words in John 14-16 opened up to me the vision of a biblically-shaped ministry.

Here Jesus describes what life will be like for his followers when he returns to the Father. At the heart of these chapters are sayings about the Holy Spirit, that we know as the Paraclete (14:16-18; 14:26-27; 15:26-27; 16:7-15) after the Greek *patakletos* used uniquely for the Holy Spirit in them. These sayings speak of Jesus sending the Holy Spirit saying, "another Advocate, to be with you forever" (John 14:16 NRSV), to continue his witness life in the world through the lives of disciples like you and me.

Note: The reader may find the concepts of this chapter expanded in chapters 6, 9 & 10 of *When Jesus Said Good-bye* by Frank G. Carver. Copyright 1996 by Beacon Hill Press of Kansas City. Available from the publisher.

First I examine one promise preceding the first saying, Jesus' intriguing words in 14:12, and second I will explore the third Paraclete saying, Jesus' explicit promise concerning the Holy Spirit in 15:26-27.

John 14:12

"Very truly, I tell you, the one who believes in me will do also
the works that I do and, in fact, will do greater works than these,
because I am going to the Father."

Jesus' promise in 14:12 is staggering indeed; it both attracts and intimidates the hearer. Jesus is speaking about our ministry in the world as the Holy Spirit continues Jesus' life through our lives. *We have both the same ministry as Jesus and a greater ministry than His.*

The Spirit's prophecy is fulfilled as he enables us to live out Jesus' own incarnate ministry in the world, "the one who believes in me will also do the works that I do." Our ministry is a continuation of his. We are not merely to do the same *kind* of works as his; we are to perform the *same* works—his works. It is a subtle but real difference.

What does Jesus mean by "the works that I do"? What is the essence of Jesus' ministry, the spiritual realities that his works signify? The essence of Jesus' ministry was encountering those of his generation with the real promise of the Father. It was bringing men and women to faith in the Son of God, "I am in the Father, and the Father is in me" (14:10).

At Jesus' healing of the sick man at the pool of Bethesda on the Sabbath (5:1-15), a life-giving activity took place. "Just as the Father raises the dead and gives them life, so also the Son gives life to whomever he wishes" (5:21).

This life-giving activity was at the same time as "a judging activity." "The Father judges no one but has given all judgment to the Son" (5:22). Jesus' critics were pronouncing judgment on themselves by their reactions to Jesus' healing on the Sabbath. Jesus' reply to their criticism, "My Father is still working, and I also am working" (5:17), explains that he is only doing what his Father is doing.

The multi-level activity of Jesus is seen most vividly in his greatest of works, the work of the cross. There he gives life to all who believe. At the cross men and women who reject the one great life-giving work of God bring themselves under final judgment even in the present (John 3:17-21).

What is the nature of our ministry within this multi-level continual activity of Jesus in the world? Where is the heart of our service? What are *we* accomplishing for Christ, in and through all we are doing for the church, on the job, in the classroom, where we live, and with our friends, every moment of every day? For *we* are the church in ministry!

The truth is that our living in continuity with the works of Jesus, leads men and women inevitably in the direction of wholeness of life or of darkness of life. We are either bringing healing through light-illumined belief to others, or we are leaving them tightly imprisoned, alienated from God, and hardened in the darkness of unbelief. This life-giving and judging effect of our lives "in continuity with the life of Jesus in the world" takes place as we, like Jesus (5:15), simply trust in the Father. "Very truly I tell you, the Son can do nothing on his own but only what he sees the Father doing" (5:19).

Our lives are continuing the life of Jesus when we believe properly and when we love adequately like Jesus when he said, "Stand up, take your mat and walk" (v. 8). As a contemporary scholar has concluded, the Johannine conception of ministry is

> grounded in the belief that God is love and his revelation is the expression of that love. To believe, to live in and by the light of God's revelation in Jesus, is to participate in that love, to love God, Christ, and one's brothers and sisters in the faith. . . . If there are specialized ministries, they must be grounded in this fundamental ministry. (Smith 224)

In the Gospel of John "the hallmark of ministry is self-giving love, in remembrance of Christ" (Black 35).

In John 14:12, Jesus also said that future disciples "will do greater works than these" as the Holy Spirit continues his life in the world. Our works will be greater than his as disciples extend the work of Jesus throughout the world and down through the ages. The incarnation of the Word was limited to one man within the space of one small country and to one brief human life, conditioned by one person's physical and psychic strength.

I reflect on all the ministries of the students who have been through my classrooms over thirty-five years, where they have been and what they have done. They are a mere sample of the Holy Spirit's existence everywhere in space and time, geographically and historically, unlimited in its energies.

Our ministry is also greater in effect because the works of Jesus during his lifetime had only minimal results. The apostles were to gather a greater host; "look around you, and see how the fields are ripe for harvesting" (4:35).

The incarnate ministry of Jesus by any contemporary "success" criteria was a failure, if you cut off the impact of Jesus' ministry at the moment of his death. His disciples were eleven scattered and disillusioned men accompanied by a few faithful women!

At the moment of his death Jesus' work was unfulfilled. Jesus said "greater works . . . because I am going to the Father." His death and resurrection inaugurate a new order in which the Holy Spirit carries on Jesus' ministry with new clarity and effectiveness. "It is to your advantage that I go away, for if I do not go away, the Advocate will not come to you; but if I go, I will send him to you" (16:7).

Here is the fascinating and thrilling paradox of ministry; not until this point can Jesus' works be evident in the works of his disciples. "And I, when I am lifted up from the earth, will draw all people to myself" (12:32-33).

Only after being lifted up to die on a cross, only after his subsequent glorification is Jesus able to reap the full harvest of his ministry, the witness of the Spirit through his disciples. Jesus' pattern of success is through death and resurrection. Jesus' reply to the Greeks' request of Philip, "Sir, we wish to see Jesus" (John 12:21) explains: "Very truly, I tell you, unless a grain of wheat falls into the earth and dies, it remains just a single grain; but if it dies, it bears much fruit" (12:24).

So it is with our ministries and the ministry of the institutional church. Because of his death and resurrection Jesus is now at work in our ministry of discipleship, accomplishing the work of our Father God! This truth Jesus has described for us in parabolic fashion, "I am the vine, you are the branches. Those who abide in me and I in them bear much fruit, because apart from me you can do nothing" (15:5). "Fruit" is essentially bringing people into the presence of God as our presence by the Spirit is his presence. Openness to us then is life-giving, and rejection of us may be the rejection of the Spirit who is present to them in us, a movement in the direction of death.

John 15:26-27

"When the Advocate comes whom I will send to you from the Father, the Spirit of truth who comes from the Father, he will testify on my behalf. You are also to testify because you have been with me from the beginning."

The second promise of Jesus to his disciples that we wish to probe brings us directly to the role of the Holy Spirit in ministry. The Holy Spirit brings Jesus to us; he witnesses to us concerning Jesus. It is by this same Spirit that we witness to him and thus continue his ministry.

Jesus' first disciples had been with him "from the beginning." They lived with the earthly Jesus all through his ministry. We too live with the incarnate Jesus as we live in the Scriptures of the New Testament, the inspired record of Jesus' ministry in the flesh.

Jesus presents us with the biblical essence of what it means to be a witness in the world. The Holy Spirit's role simply teaches us Jesus is the foundation. He is the Spirit of truth who quickens the disciples' understanding of Jesus who said "I am . . . the truth" (14:6). In the Gospel of John, Jesus is the one who came to reveal what was true. As "the only son," he was "full of grace and truth" (1:14), the one through whom "grace and truth came" (1:17).

In continuing the ministry of Jesus, the Holy Spirit will guide disciples "into all truth" (16:13). All that Jesus brought into the world in his ministry, the Spirit opens up to the believer. As Jesus in his ministry did "nothing on his own" but only what he saw "the Father doing" (5:19), likewise the Holy Spirit in 16:13 "will not speak on his own," but will speak only "whatever he hears." So, he will speak "all the truth" of the revelation of God that has taken place in Jesus.

In John 16:13, Jesus also says of the Holy Spirit, "He will declare to you the things that are to come." His promise to us is that in each new historical situation, the work of Jesus and the truth of the gospel are disclosed anew.

This is how the Holy Spirit continues the work of Jesus. First, the Holy Spirit interprets the life and death of Jesus for his disciples and declares a new and greater intimacy with God, ushered in by His departure to the Father. In like manner he illumines the disciples' written memory of Jesus for us in the New Testament Gospels. With the Spirit's help we understand the Scriptures as they testify to Jesus and interpret who and what he is for the unique situations of our lives now! He illumines their truth to us as the risen Christ did to those on the Emmaus road, "were not our hearts burning within us while he was talking to us on the road, while he was opening the Scriptures to us" (Luke 24:32).

The witness of the Holy Spirit to Jesus in and through our lives is basic to the Holy Spirit's witness through the Church to the world. "You are also to testify because you have been with me from the beginning" (15:27). The stress in verses 26-27 is significant, "the Advocate . . . will testify on my behalf. . . . You also are to testify." Seen side by side these two sentences indicate that the Holy Spirit is the Spirit of Christian proclamation.

The witness of the Spirit and our witness are both involved as Jesus makes himself known to the world through the Church. We witness through a careful and consistent attention to the Holy Scriptures, the tradition of the Church, "you have been with me from the beginning." Jesus said earlier to his disciples that the Holy Spirit will "remind you of all that I have said to you" (14:26).

As in 1 John 2:24, "Let what you heard from the beginning abide in you," that is, remember the truth about Jesus, the apostolic witness to Christ. There is no way to effective ministry apart from living with the incarnate Jesus. Our primary access to him is through the written Word of God, our canonical Old and New Testaments. We can learn *about* the Bible until the end of time, but unless we *live in* it, there will be little effect on the quality of our witness life. We need to draw water from the deep well of our own personal reflection on the Scriptures.

We are like the New Testament Peter. Only after he had walked, talked, and lived day and night with the enfleshed Jesus, was Peter able to bear witness to Jesus as "the Christ, the Son of the living God" (Matt. 16:16).

And to this confession Jesus responded, "Blessed are you, Simon Barjonas, because flesh and blood did not reveal this to you, but My Father who is in heaven" (16:17).

We minister as we live day in and day out with the incarnate Jesus as mediated to us through our application of mind and heart to the whole of the Scriptures as written. Through this process the Holy Spirit will speak in a transforming and consistent manner to us informing and empowering our witness life in the world. By definition "Christian" proclamation is "biblical." Our preaching will only be truly biblical when the Bible governs its content and when the function of the sermon is analogous to that of the biblical text: "preaching is biblical when it imparts a Bible-shaped word in a Bible-like way" (Keck 106).

We minister second by our utter reliance on the Spirit of truth; "when the Advocate comes . . . , the Spirit of truth, . . . he will testify on my behalf" (15:26).

It is the Holy Spirit who convicts the world (16:8) as he continues the work of Jesus. This is the thrust of the final Paraclete saying, 16:5-11, where we see how our witness actually "works" or "bears fruit" in the world.

The Church is to the present world what Jesus was to his world. In 16:7-11, Jesus gives us "a picture of the Church's ministry in progress, drawn as graphically as the description of Jesus' earthly ministry earlier in the gospel"(Sanders 352). These verses depict what the Holy Spirit actually does as he goes on the offensive, when through our witness he reveals Jesus to the world. "Nevertheless I tell you the truth: it is to your advantage that I go away, for if I do not go away, the Advocate will not come to you; but if I go, I will send him to you. And when he comes, he will prove the world wrong about sin, and righteousness and judgment" (16:7-8).

What is meant by the "sin, and righteousness, and judgment" with reference to which the Holy Spirit will "*expose* the world and *demonstrate its error*" (Beasley-Murray 281)? Disclosed in the Spirit's revelation is "the true meaning of the standards and values current in the world," which "means at the same time disclosing who is the sinner, who the victor, and who it is that is judged" (Bultmann 563).

We witness as the life of Christ flows out from our lives by the Holy Spirit. When we in the Christian community allow the risen Jesus to live his resurrected life through us, the Holy Spirit will bear witness to us concerning Jesus. Thus through us the Church "will prove the world wrong about sin and righteousness and judgment."

The promise of Jesus inspires our hope for a ministry that is truly biblical, for a witness that is truly his. "Receive the Holy Spirit. If you forgive the sins of any, their sins have forgiven them; if you retain the sins of any, they have been retained" (20:22-23). The world will *know* when the Holy Spirit reveals the truth of Christ *to us* in such radiating force that the Church confronts the world with convincing power. Henri Nouwen, reflecting on the witness of St. Antony, assures us that "when we are filled with God's merciful presence, we can do nothing other than minister because our whole being witnesses to the light that has come into the darkness"(Nouwen 37).

Such a quality of ministry is out there for you and me as we dare to let the Spirit of Christ shape us by the Word of God. Over my thirty-five years of teaching I have attempted to instill a vision of a biblically authentic ministry in my students. It is a vision that is immersed in the Scriptures and ministers in submission to the Word. The Holy Spirit has promised to always anoint, not *our* words, but *God's Word* with his own life-encountering presence.

Life can get heavy at times, so when I enter the sanctuary as a worshipper on Sunday morning, I desire to be brought into the presence of a holy and awesome God. I want to hear the voice of the Spirit through the Word as my pastor, who has sought to hear the biblical text to the best of his/her ability, seeks to share what is heard in submission to its authority. When that happens, I leave the sanctuary convicted and transformed, refreshed and empowered to be Christian another week.

As a minister, what better thing do you have to tell me than what is in the Scriptures? What is more important than to encounter me with the presence of the Holy One in judgment and in grace? If you will lay open to my heart the witness of the biblical text, it will be the most significant hour of my week.

WORKS CITED

Beasley-Murray, George R. *John.* Vol. 36 of *Word Biblical Commentary.* 51 vols. Waco, TX: Word, 1987.

Black, C. Clifton. "Christian Ministry in Johannine Perspective." *Interpretation* 44 (Jan. 1990): 29-41.

Bultmann, Rudolf. *The Gospel of John: A Commentary.* Trans. George R. Beasley-Murray. Philadelphia: Westminster P, 1971.

Keck, Leander E. *The Bible in the Pulpit: The Renewal of Biblical Preaching.* Nashville: Abingdon, 1978.

Metzger, Bruce M. and Roland E. Murphy, eds. *Bible: New Revised Standard Version.* New York: Oxford UP, 1991.

Nouwen, Henri. *The Way of the Heart: Desert Spirituality and Contemporary Ministry.* New York: Seabury P, 1981.

Sanders, Joseph N. and B. A. Mastin. *A Commentary on the Gospel of John: Black New Testament Commentaries.* London: Adam and Charles Black, 1968.

Smith, D. Moody. "Theology and Ministry in John." *A Biblical Basis for Ministry*. Ed . Earl E. Shelp and Ronald Sutherland. Philadelphia: Westminster P, 1981.

Carver, Frank, *Ph.D. Dr. Carver currently teaches theology and Bible courses at the European Nazarene Bible College in Switzerland after a 35-year academic and administrative career at Point Loma Nazarene College. While serving as professor of biblical theology and Greek as well as directing Graduate Studies in Religion, Carver established himself as a respected writer. His published works include two books, numerous articles in Christian journals and contributions to the Beacon Bible Commentary and Wycliffe Bible Encyclopedia.*

CHAPTER SIX

PRAYER:
THE CONTINUING RESPONSE

Jim Mullins

Make decisions and God works through human minds.
Make discoveries and humans work through the Divine Mind.

Accepting God's call to ministry is not the end of a road, but merely the beginning of an adventure. Just as one responds to God's initial call by acceptance, so one also responds by affirmation to God's further promptings. It does not take long to learn that the initial call by God is not enough to guide, sustain or protect one during current opportunities. To solely lean on one's past call to ministry is to insure one's failure in present ministry. A lifelong commitment to faithful listening, trusting and obeying the immediate leadings of God's Spirit is the essence of fruitful ministry. The continuing positive response to God is called *prayer*, hence the title of this chapter.

What is prayer? Is it the skillfully crafted sequence of words to open a session of a legislature? Is it the anguished groaning next to the bed of a dying family member? Is it the repetition of wonderful words written long ago? Is it the frenzied outpouring of thoughts at the end of an emotionally charged church service? Is it the kneeling child's last words before climbing into bed? Is it the tortured screams of the abused? Is it the silence of watching the sun set at evening? Is it the conversation between a person and God? Yes, prayer is all of these and more.

For the purpose of this chapter, however, "prayer" is defined as "a lifting of the mind and heart to God" (Green 27). This will help us to understand that God is apart from us and yet approachable. God is neither an extension of our personality nor the sum total of all our hopes and experiences or fears. God is God. This definition of prayer will also lead us to understand that prayer involves work on our part. Prayer does not just happen. It is a conscious effort. ". . . [A]nyone who comes to him must believe that he exists and that he rewards those who earnestly seek him" (Heb. 11:6 NIV). The total person relates to God in prayer. It is not activity of just mind *or* heart *or* body. It is an activity of mind *and* heart *and* body. Albert E. Day adds

> Prayer's function is to set God at the center of your attention: to open yourself to the illumination of His knowledge about yourself and your situation. . . . The decisive question is this, always, "Is my consciousness, simply, humbly, but wholly directed toward and centered upon God?" (44-45)

How do we center our consciousness on God? How can we lift mind and heart and body to God? How can the Divine occupy our attention? Must we all live in a convent or monastery so that we can pray? I suggest three simple ways of praying that are possible to everyone involved in ministry.

Spending Time With God

Be still, and know that I am God (Ps. 46:10 NRSV)

I believe that the first task of prayer is simply to be with God, to devote some time to solitude, silence and stillness. Jesus underscored the importance of this kind of praying when he called his disciples. "And he appointed twelve, whom he also named apostles, to be with him, and to be sent out to proclaim the message" (Mark 3:14 NRSV). While many wish to rush out to fulfill their call to ministry, Jesus wanted his followers to spend time with him first. Jesus' followers were busy proclaiming the message but only after they spent sufficient time with Jesus.

The time spent with God does not have to be formal, verbal, or structured in any way. It seems to many that a daily period of "wasting time with God" is very effective. Thomas H. Green tells of a boyhood memory:

> Jimmy was a simple man, of little formal education. Each day, when returning from work, he stopped in the church and sat in the back for several minutes. The parish priest noticed the regularity of Jimmy's visits and his fervor. He wondered just what a simple man like Jimmy did during these visits. One day he asked him what happened. Jimmy replied, "Nothing much, Father. I just say, 'Jesus, it's Jimmy.' And he says, 'Jimmy, it's Jesus.' And we're happy together." (19)

A busy physician I know has a similar pattern of praying. After rising each morning he jogs for several miles. When he returns home, he pours himself a cup of coffee and sits on the back porch while his body cools down from exercise. He acknowledges God's presence and sits quietly for a few minutes with God. The time spent alone with God each morning makes the difference in his days.

When I was pastoring in San Juan Capistrano, I noticed a great blue heron flying into the field next to the church each morning. I began to make it my practice to take a cup of coffee and stand outside the office and watch the bird seek for food. I invited God to share the moment with me. I spent my "coffee break" each day with God and a great blue heron. I cannot remember any great visions or insights. I do not think I said anything at all. Nothing much was accomplished except that I realized daily that God was with me. When I moved to pastor another church, my life seemed depleted until I developed a new way of spending time with God.

Standing Together with God

"And I sought for anyone among them who would repair the wall and stand in the breach before me on behalf of the land, so that I would not destroy it, but I found no one." (Ezek. 22:30 NRSV)

I am indebted to Dennis Kinlaw for a new insight into Genesis 18 (41-43). God, along with two others, visited Abraham and talked about the fulfillment of God's promise to him. They informed Abraham that his son would arrive in about a year. The others left for Sodom; and the alternate reading in the NIV says: but the *Lord* remained standing before Abraham (Gen. 18:22). After Abraham pled for the salvation of Sodom and Gomorrah, God left. "When the LORD had finished speaking with Abraham, he left, and Abraham returned home" (Gen. 18:33 NIV).

Could it possibly be that as God looks on this plane, God wishes to have someone stand alongside and pray for the world's salvation? This is certainly the case with Jesus, who while wrestling with his future death on the cross, asked the disciples to pray with him, to stay awake with him (Luke 22:39-46).

I believe that there are many times during ministry when God will prompt his son or daughter to wake up and stand while God agonizes over the world. Praying for the world apparently is not done alone, even by God. Many times a minister will simply ache for people, nations, nature, and relationships. I have come to believe that this aching does not come from the minister but from God. It has been the experience of some that they do not even know why they ache, only that God is asking them to stand for a while.

Sharing Ministry With God

Then the king said to me, "What do you request?" So I prayed to the God of heaven. Then I said . . . (Neh. 2:4,5a NRSV)

Another way of praying is to simply keep God informed of what is happening in your life and ministry *as it happens*. Some think that prayer should only occur prior to and away from the actual ministry. While that kind of preparation is good, I also believe that keeping God constantly apprised of our situation is very effective. I remember the first time I saw the musical, *Fiddler on the Roof*. I was amazed and challenged by the way Tevye maintained a continuous conversation with God. Every event in Tevye's life, good or bad, small or large, personal or communal was shared with God.

This constant sharing with God seems to be Jesus' pattern of prayer as portrayed in the Gospel of Luke. He mentions Jesus praying seven times. After his baptism, Jesus was praying on the shore when the Holy Spirit descended on him (3:21). Before choosing the twelve who became his disciples, Jesus spent the night praying to God (6:12). After praying, Jesus asked his disciples who he was (9:18). Jesus was praying on the mountain when he was transfigured (9:28-29). The disciples asked Jesus to teach them to pray after watching him pray (11:1). Before going to the cross, Jesus agonized in prayer at Gethsemane (22:39-46). Perhaps the most telling statement regarding the prayer life of Jesus is found in 5:16, "From time to time he would withdraw to lonely places for prayer" (NEB). It seems to me that Jesus maintained a constant two-way communication with God concerning all the events of his life.

One way that I share my ministry with God, I call *consolation-desolation*. It takes me about five minutes each evening. I ask the desolation question first, "What took life from me today?" I then ask the consolation question, "What gave life to me today?" Sometimes I write this in a journal. Sometimes I share it with my wife or sons. Sometimes I just ask and answer the questions in my mind. I believe that I go to sleep easier each evening because I have shared my ministry with God.

Conclusion

It is my profound belief that prayer is the relational connection among God, self, others and the world. Prayer gives us strength for both personal and professional integrity. Prayer is the continuing response to God in ministry.

A Prayer:
> *God, you have called me to this way of serving you.*
> *I need you to be with me because I cannot do this alone.*
> *Help me in the easy days ahead to remember you.*
> *Help me in the difficult days ahead to trust you, to believe that you know what you are doing with my life.*

*Please prompt me to spend time with you daily, getting to know you and my
world and myself.*
Allow me to share with you all the times of my life.
*And Lord, when you are hurting over the world we humans have made
and need someone to stand with you, I want to be with you.*
Thank you for accepting my response to your call. Amen.

WORKS CITED

The Bible. New International Version.

The Bible. New Revised Standard Version.

Day, Albert Edward. *An Autobiography of Prayer.* New York: Harper, 1952.

Green, Thomas H. *Opening to God: A Guide to Prayer.* Notre Dame, IN: Ave Maria P, 1977.

Kinlaw, Dennis F. *Preaching in the Spirit.* Grand Rapids, MI: Francis Asbury P, 1985.

The New English Bible. Oxford UP and Cambridge UP, 1961 (NT) and 1970 (OT).

SUGGESTED READING

Green, Thomas H. *When the Well Runs Dry.* Notre Dame, IN: Ave Maria P, 1995.

—. *Darkness in the Marketplace.* Notre Dame, IN: Ave Maria P, 1981.

—. *Drinking from a Dry Well.* Notre Dame, IN: Ave Maria P, 1995.

Leech, Kenneth. *True Prayer.* Glenview, IL: Harpercollins, 1986.

Maloney, George A. *Inward Stillness.* Denville, NJ: Dimension Books, 1976.

—. *Prayer of the Heart.* Notre Dame, IN: Ave Maria P, 1995.

Mullins, Jim, *D.Min. Dr. Mullins is the Senior Pastor at Heights First Church
of the Nazarene in Albuquerque, New Mexico and is an adjunct professor of
Christianity at the Nazarene Indian Bible College. He has also pastored churches in
Missouri, California, and Maine. Mullins was named a President's Ministerial
Fellow at Point Loma Nazarene College for Spring 1995.*

PART TWO

CONNECTING WITH GOD'S COMMUNITY FOR MINISTRY

*T*he church is to be the transformed community where ministers are affirmed, equipped and empowered for servanthood. This section offers a dynamic profile of the church in which God's grace breaks through the barriers of color, creeds, and cultures. The following chapters explain a number of underlying social forces that are shaking the traditions and membership make-up of denominations. They also address the ongoing challenges regarding men and women working side by side as partners in ministry.

CHAPTER SEVEN

THE CHURCH:
GOD'S MINISTERING SERVANT
IN OUR NEIGHBORHOOD

David Whitelaw

I kgopoleng Molebatsi looked out at the world from 2555 Masao Drive, Dobsonville, Soweto, Republic of South Africa, in the 1970s. His mother was guardian of a household of diverse and difficult people and wife to a school princi-pal whose vision of a better life held the "family" together. Twelve to fifteen people normally occupied the tiny, four-room, thirty foot by twenty-four foot brick dwelling, located in a drab and dusty township, with no flowers or grass to relieve the reality of a community structured by apartheid social engineering. Ikgopoleng, a Christian believer, was leader of his high school student council and a restless but determined pioneer on the pathway of grace and faith, love and hope. Between the fearsome alternatives of hate and servility, compliance and anger, he committed himself to a journey to seek a neighborhood of acceptance, a brotherhood of accountability, and a family of sisters and brothers characterized by the peace and justice of the reign and rule of God. Above all, he wanted to be part of that community of Christ which is the church of all times and places. He planted a ten foot by four foot patch of green grass in front of his mother's house—the only colorful sign in the neighborhood, of hope and life and faith—where everything around tasted and smelled of despair, discour-agement and indeed, death. That is where I met him, where he challenged me to become a part of that provisional order of God's kingdom.

It is Easter 1996 as I write these words. It was Good Friday 1980, when I participated in a three-hour Vigil of the Cross in the northern suburbs in Johannesburg, South Africa, and quietly responded to the poignant beau-ty of sacred scripture, song and homily as Christ's Seven Words from the Cross were proclaimed. Nothing, it seemed, could or should break the solemn meditation on the life and death and resurrection of Jesus, the Christ.

My quest to draw near to the Jesus of the cross was gently, firmly inter-rupted. I could not escape the disturbing intuition that I could not find Christ in that setting. I began to suspect that his cross and his passion were erected and enacted elsewhere. Where? . . . I wondered.

Ikgopoleng (his friends called him "Moses" or "Mos," a family name) came to mind, a restless, insistent, beckoning shadow. I left my pew, drove the few miles to Dobsonville, only "around the corner" really (part of my neighborhood) but "the other side of my world," as I was to discover. I located the patch of green grass, the humble Molebatsi dwelling, and Mos. I began my journey with him to find a new place in a "rough neighborhood" (Crocker). What we found was the graced space of God's new neighborhood of the kingdom.

This Church is one, holy, catholic and apostolic in its classical definition. It is God's humble servant, the bride and body of Christ to enflesh Christ's ministry in the world (I Cor. 12:27; Eph. 5:25-27). It is a Trinitarian community created by grace, made alive through faith, nurtured in love, energized by hope, embodying the obedience of Jesus Christ to God the Father (Eph. 3:14-21; Phil. 2:5-11). It is God's new order, a beloved invader of the old orders of this world. Its members are guerrillas of grace (Loder). The church is God's "emergent new order" where "nascent covenant-communities" of the kingdom are birthed in "neighborhoods of grace" marked by God's holiness, the splendor of "ordinary people" living holy lives.

I invite you to take a journey into the twenty-first century, to find your own path to ministry in this new order. As Jesus claimed, this kingdom is right here—next door (Mark 1:15), and the entrance to it is through repentance and faith. Here there are four searching questions for the pilgrim-traveler: *Where in the world is my neighbor? Do I have time for my neighbor? What in the world shall we do together? What is the outcome of our journey?*

Where in the World is My Neighbor?

Jesus had a conversation with a lawyer seeking eternal life. He signposted the journey: "You shall love the Lord your God with all your heart, soul, mind and strength, and your neighbor as yourself." The lawyer responded, "Well, who is my neighbor?" (Luke 10:27-9) or rephrased, "Where in the world is my neighbor?"

Since Cain and Abel, brothers who became enemies, persons struggle to create a safe space for neighbors, for sisters and brothers in which the whole human family is welcome not because of blood relationship, class kinship, religious affiliation, or ethnic identity. The welcome mat is put out with an understanding and acceptance that we share a world of graced space, with our common origins in the parenthood of a loving Creator. Our neighbor is found next door on the common ground of a shared humanity. This is a level place where one does not descend nor condescend to the other.

The nature and calling of the Church is to provide scaffolding for the construction, not so much of buildings, or programs, or strategies, but of persons who discover each other in neighborhoods marked by the habits and practices of Christlikeness (Fowl and Jones 1-2). For this to occur, the Church needs to recover her ability to hear and recognize the voice that calls her. She is a community of *memory* and *hope*, the twin keys of Christian identity. It is a community characterized by obedience to a voice, like the call to Abram, "Leave your family and your homeland and go to a place which I will show you" (Gen. 12:1-2). The community of the people of God is formed by pilgrims hearing and responding to a voice that cannot be duplicated nor recorded (Nouwen 153). The journey ends with a wedding feast, with God coming home to God's people (Rev. 21:1-4).

The Church is a "way of being in the world." Jesus called people out (*ek+kaleo*) to become participants in a new community called the Church (*ekklesia*). Those so called are to embody the life and being of the kingdom in this world, to be God's "prototype" or "garden/seedbed" (I Cor. 3:5-9) where his kingdom purposes are experimentally tested. John D. Zizioulas of the University of Glasgow captures this in a fresh understanding of the early church and Orthodox tradition in his *Being as Communion*: "The Church is not simply an institution. She is a 'mode of existence,' *a way of being* . . . bound to the very being of God" (15). The Church, like a steeple, points beyond particular places and times to the destiny (*eschaton)* or the goal of the kingdom. An apt metaphor is that of a little bird, poised on the rooftop of a church, between heaven and earth, a fragile fragment of life symbolizing the "already, not yet" of the reign of God. God's kingdom has already come but it is not yet consummated. The divine intent is to set up home with the people of God (Rev. 21:3), whose members are "resident aliens" in this world (Hauerwas and Willimon; Phil. 3:20).

Moses and I were to discover that we too were resident aliens. The South African government provided Moses with citizenship documents for a "homeland" (called Bophuthatswana) over 200 miles away, a "home" that he had never seen nor visited. In turn, I chose to become a "resident alien" by accepting an offer to serve in the United States for a time, and so receive a "green card" guaranteeing permanent residence in a country hospitable to strangers and immigrants. In the dawning realization that we were both resident aliens, we discovered each other as neighbors. We did this by relocating ourselves in relation to Christ rather than in relation to the cultures and society where we lived.

David Tracy says that at the center of Christianity stands not a timeless truth, nor a principle, nor even a cause, but an event and a person—Jesus of Nazareth experienced and confessed as the Christ (317). Luther referred to Christ Jesus as an "Alien Word" spoken from "outside" (Oberman 226). In Augustine's terms this Word is God's sacra-ment or "visible word" of grace. Spirit and structure are connected in a sacramental view of the world. It is the constant tendency of the church to reduce this word to a text, creed or confession and to constrict the arena of grace (the entire cosmos) to the structures of institutional management where the word of the text and even the sacraments are regarded as the possessions of the Church. The marginalized Christ watches from the periphery of our attention where we scarcely notice that he is rebuilding God's kingdom in new neighborhoods that reclaim the fullness of the text and the world in the spaciousness of grace (See Pacini 174; Van Beeck 214).

Sidney E. Mead captured something of this when he wrote *The Lively Experiment: The Shaping of Christianity in America.* Churchly traditions from Europe accustomed to cramped quarters and religious persecution (for example, both Lutherans and Catholics persecuted Anabaptists) found more space in the New World to create new models (voluntarism and denominationalism) but were always short on time. An African might ask, "Are Americans always in a hurry?" This prompts a new question:

Do I Have Time for my Neighbor?

Neither Moses nor I had time for each other at the outset. We lived too far apart. The currents of our communities swept us past each other. However, at a certain point chronology was overtaken by a *kairos* moment, as if the whole of the past and the future was captured in one Olympic golden "moment in time."

Theological and biblical ways of speaking about time provided us with fresh insights into our journey, and as a result we made time for each other in new ways. *Kairos* introduced the ideas of both crisis and opportunity into the frame of ordinary *chronos,* or clock time.

The two South African fellow-travelers were learning to discover something of this new order of living in a dangerous neighborhood. They were finding a new shared identity as "resident aliens." They became caught up in the tide of events that rudely awakened both to the dialectic of history, of continuity and crisis. In 1985, the controversial *Kairos Document* was published and created a storm of protest in the way it mirrored racism institutionalized in church and society in the country. It came at a time of national emergency and terrifying violence. It had almost apocalyptic overtones of judgment on the peoples of South Africa.

Christian ministry is a balancing act with time, like walking a tightrope, or better, living on a threshold. There is a technical theological word for this, the edge or the *eschaton.* Ministry for the kingdom requires a new order of living—by crossing the threshold at our feet that may seem like a canyon precipice. Ministers may be called doorkeepers of the kingdom (Ps.84:10). They are pathfinders who illumine the way ahead by wise and practical use of the Word (this is one sense of the words of Paul to Timothy in II Tim. 2:15, that ministers are to "rightly divide the word of truth," clearing away the undergrowth of misunderstanding).

Ministry is the ordering of the whole life of the people of God in what we may call "Space Time" so that their work is the worship of God (Acts 13:1-6; *leitourgos*, the work of the people, the *laos*, in a liturgy of life). This is an exciting discovery when a believer, a pilgrim in *chronos* time, encounters his neighbor through a *kairos* or crisis awareness that they are in fact fellow-travelers crossing a threshold or boundary into the new order of the kingdom.

How may we re-think our use of ordinary, *chronos* time? Sojourners like John Wesley (who believed in "improving the present moment") have provided a model of response to critical transitions in human experience. For him faith was the fullest embracing of the present moment for the kingdom. This was the essence of a lively faith. His favorite, concise definition of the Christian religion was that it is "living faith." By living, he meant the "true, scriptural, experimental religion," the faith that works by love, as a result of a living encounter with God. He did not mean "Jesus-in-my-heart solitary faith" nor "if it works for you that's OK, religion." Living faith means to be *connected* with the living continuity of Christian faith down through the centuries. Our ordinary *chronos* moments, disconnected, appear trivial and meaningless. Mildred Bangs Wynkoop, Nazarene theologian, has reminded us that continuity of grace is one of the defining marks of the Wesleyan tradition (77-98). This means that Christian ministry is carried out in a loving, creative tension between chronological time (continuity) and *kairos* time (crisis, urgency) where the dialectical imagination (calm, rational, analytical, practical thinking) and the analogical imagination (intuitive, synthetic vision of the whole picture) must be fully engaged in partnership. John Wesley teaches us then to use the present moment by seeing its connections with the kingdom more clearly.

How may we re-think our responses to crises—to *kairos* moments of danger and opportunity? The Christian church is a community living in the *dialectic* of history, connected down through the centuries with the first believers, but living in all the contingency and tension of a real world of tests and triumphs, of breathtaking beauty and wrenching tragedies, of loving communities but also, at times, of groups in brutal conflict (Bosnia, Ireland, Somalia, Kwazulu-South Africa). Martin Luther helps us here. In 1525, the German peasants revolted; the Black Plague caused the death of one-third of the people in Europe; and the Muslim invaders advanced to the gates of Vienna. People were alarmed and feared that this was God's *kairos* moment of final Judgment and of Christ's return. His friends asked, "What will you do, Brother Martin?" Pausing a moment, he replied, "I will go out and plant a tree, and take a wife" (Katherine of Bora), which he did that same year!

Phineas Bresee, founder of the Church of the Nazarene, also illustrates this connection between *chronos* and *kairos* time. He repeatedly claimed that if he had only ten years left to minister, he would spend five years preparing, in careful education, and then accomplish more in the remaining five than if he had immediately moved into ministry. John Wesley too is said to have claimed that if he knew Christ's return was to be on a particular day, he would simply check his diary and complete his schedule in a perfectly normal, "ordinary" way.

How may we then make time for our neighbor in light of the end, the eschaton, the kingdom of God? Making time for people is often not what we regard as part of our normal business. Our "busyness" often programs us into so-called ministry activities that take us away from the ordinary, as well as special, events of people. Ministry, Jesus style, means making room for the unexpected, setting aside "busyness" to make room and time for our neighbor (Erwin).

The Church is the community above all others that is asked to live simply in the midst of complexity, open to these kinds of tensions in time. Those who are alert find grace sneaking in along with severe pressures. This grace is imperceptible to those who see only ordinary events in their ordinary contexts.

Ministry is like living on the edge, in tension between past and future. There the NOW of faith in the present moment becomes possible. The Church is a meeting-place for people who are gathered together in ordinary *chronos* time in the name of Christ, and the extraordinary *eschaton* of the kingdom of God. Faith is the capacity for openness to this ultimate purpose of God that transcends history. It is also the capacity for openness to one another in human community. "The Christian is hospitable, one who welcomes, one who receives, one who accepts, others" (Paoli 8). The church is a community of living faith, living "between the times" as it were, but open to the profoundly two-fold nature of crisis and continuity. The *immediacy* of grace, which makes faith possible *now*, requires both immediate accessibility to God and mediated structures for connections of the Spirit. Our third question is as follows:

What in the World Should We Be Doing Together?

The real task of the Church is to make God's redeeming love in Jesus Christ present for broken people in a hurting world. What in the world should we be doing in the church? What in the world are we doing if it is not the reconstruction of persons in the world for becoming fully human? This happens when the connections (the fiber and sinew of new relationships) for being filled with the Spirit of God exist in human communities that are being transformed toward Christlikeness. A remarkable thing happened in South Africa in the late 1980s. In the midst of violence, blood and tears, persons of various classes, ethnic, social and religious backgrounds, began to notice each other's pain and anger, trauma and tears. Mos and I, our family and friends, attended to each other in new ways. We carved out new spaces and times to meet and converse. The most astonishing to us was the rediscovery of what is perhaps the most obvious activity of human beings; we began to "break bread together" in each other's home (Acts 2:46).

A new quest for community (New Testament writers called this *koinonia,* or fellowship) began in that divided land. The stable, pyramidical structures of church, school and state showed signs of crumbling and cracks in the old rigidities. To change the metaphor, some people sought new life-rafts for the now dangerous journey, like safe refuges on a river in flood.

Ralph Winter has documented what occurs when stable, rigid "vertical" institutional structures replace the fluid, open, horizontal, missional movements of Christian witness. What is being described here is the reverse process: when closed and institutionally defined patterns and processes of living are broken open to new, humanizing patterns of association and relationship. The construction of persons in community becomes more important than the successful functioning of organizational strategies.

Love is the real bridge of connection between human beings. Brian Gaybba speaks of *kenotic* love as the mark of Christian community (Phil. 2:1-11) and of "love as the lamp of theology." Love that dies to give birth, love that pours itself out for the other, love that gives and so finds itself again. Ministry has to do with the birth of this love through grace, which is at work in Christian communities structured to give and preserve this kind of life.

The wholeness of persons, their dignity and self-respect, is both starting point (created in grace) and destination (redeemed by grace) of such a pilgrimage in community. A Point Loma Nazarene College colleague is functioning as a pathfinder in this area. Michael Leffel explores what may be called a theology of generative love where the reconstruction of persons is described in the language of the professional psychologist (115-131). This concept enlarges our understanding of ministry to embrace the vocation of the professional psychologist.

The human community moves toward becoming authentically Christian to the degree that this regenerative love functions between persons where forgiveness and healing flow gently and powerfully in human relationships. John Wesley probably would have called this *prevenient* grace, accessible to all.

Those who seek to minister from the resources of this tradition have the forgotten strands of the Anglican tradition at their fingertips in the building of Christian community. Canon Allchin uses the hymns of Charles Wesley to demonstrate that the idea of *participation in God* is both an essential and overlooked element in the Church of England where Wesleyan roots lie. The pardoning grace of the Western tradition interwoven with the threads of empowering and purifying grace of the Eastern tradition produce a human tapestry of living connection where spirituality is recovered in the "coming to be fully human" of the community "re-membering itself" by overcoming the amnesia of a stunted memory.

The quest for spirituality may be represented in various modes at various times in the journey of the Church of Jesus Christ. David Lowes Watson documents the function of Methodist class meetings as "Covenant Discipleship Groups." He reminds us that this process of re-membering or re-appropriating the tradition of the Christian church will require a "radical inversion" whereby Christian congregations and ministers accept and affirm that in God's plan of salvation *the church comes last, not first* (34). Churches must become turned inside-out from being "safe houses" of self-preservation into "open houses" centered on Christ.

The community of love therefore is called to embody the *kenotic* love of Jesus (Phil. 2:1-11) which is turned inside-out in service to the world. In this way congregations function as "sign communities of the coming reign of God." The Pastoral Rule of Prudence and Self-Preservation gives way to the lifestyle practice of Christlike loving and living expressed in words like these:

> To witness to Jesus Christ in the world,
> and to follow his teachings through
> acts of compassion, justice, worship, and devotion,
> under the guidance of the Holy Spirit. (Watson 9)

The minister of the twenty-first century will seek models of ministry and congregational life that no one can predict with accuracy now. This requires the recognition that the Church of Jesus Christ is a mystery that will require images and analogies as much as precise definitions and descriptions. Various models will not produce one synthetic vision, or one coherent system or strategy (Dulles 9-10).

What is the Hoped-for Outcome of Our Journey?

Where does our journey into ministry in the twenty-first century lead? Robert Wuthnow has written reflections on the challenges ahead, and has documented America's new quest for community in *Sharing the Journey: Support Groups and America's New Quest for Community*. We live in a society where cultural and ideological pluralism abounds and where the failures of churches and ministers are often painfully self-evident. Is the minister of tomorrow a provider of private spirituality, a "me first" religion? Is the Christian minister a promoter of new kinds of support groups, offering care for the full range of human needs? The Christian church must go beyond this kind of support and survival community: Christ's church must be a living community of Christian hope, vision, energy and new life. My own work with sociologist John Hawthorne has led us to the formulation of the idea of the church as a "nascent covenant-community of the kingdom," an experiment in "Space Time" where the birthing of a new society is taking place. A church that is a *Christian community of hope* will find ways to birth "nascent covenant-communities" of the kingdom, in a new love affair with the Bridegroom of the Church.

Sidney Mead broke fresh ground in his generation and led the way for all those who sought a new vision of Christianity in American culture (Brauer viii). Mead affirmed a new center for the whole of religious history in America in his focus on what he saw as the incarnation of religious liberty in the Constitution. Willingness to risk, a "lively experiment," an acknowledgment of the necessity of living in hope in the face of an intractable past and dubious future: *that* is the gift he gave his contemporaries, beginning with an honest assessment of himself.

A church that is a *community of hope* is willing to live by *kenotic* love, pouring its energies into being "emergent orders of holy living" (Bassett) rather than self-preservation societies for a denomination. Phineas Bresee, guardian of the holiness tradition and pathfinder of a new order of ministry "out under the stars," was willing to put his heritage at risk in advancing into a new century one hundred years ago (Bangs). He loved to affirm the hopefulness of faith among the marginalized poor in downtown Los Angeles, as evidenced by his personal adage "the sun never sets in the morning." Carl Bangs documents that J. P. Widney and Bresee claimed that the name Church of the Nazarene linked Christ to "the great toiling, struggling, sorrowing heart of the world." It was to Jesus of Nazareth that "the world in its misery and despair turns, that it may have hope" (196).

A church which is a *community of hope* will establish "neighborhood watches" of the kingdom for the reconstruction of persons, as much or more than in-house programs. The goal of ministry in the church of all times and places is to serve as expendable, provisional, pilot projects or models of the kingdom. In a benign sense the church is a "throw-away society." (One can hardly imagine Jesus speaking of his "throw-away bride," however!) It is a temporary seed-bed for the kingdom, a mere means to kingdom ends. It is a society of resident aliens who subversively usher in the kingdom using the means and methods of grace.

A church which is a *community of hope* is a society of persons mature and secure enough in corporate identity to allow healthy processes of self-critique to occur. The kingdom of God provides what Christianity in its human, institutional embodiment requires, constant *critique* from beyond itself. The idea of the kingdom of God, however outmoded and flawed its "imperial" and "patriarchal" images may be, nevertheless provides the institutional church with the constant reminder that it must continually be expanded beyond its hardening boundaries and categories. The

Reformers loved to say, the church is *reforma semper reformanda*, reformed, always reforming.

Howard Snyder identifies *Models of the Kingdom* to help us on our journey. How do people think about the kingdom? Some say God rules the heart, others the church; some say God rules the cosmos, or human history, and still others say that here we need no monarch or kingdom. Prodded by writers like him, let us explore some options for a church and ministry seeking to live out the fullest possible embodiment of the whole purpose of God, in all times and places. We need to begin with the very particular places in which we find ourselves: A church modeled on the kingdom embodies a way of being in the world which is profoundly Trinitarian, caught up in the work of worship to God the Father, in the Name of the Son, and by the power of the Spirit. The Anglican Frederick Denison Maurice, a contemporary of Bresee and known for his passionate intensity, was described like this:

> His countenance expressed nervous, high-strung tension, as though all the various play of feelings in ordinary human nature converged, in him, towards a single focus, the declaration of the divine purpose. (xiii)

That is the focus of the journey: the purpose of the reign and rule of God, with the energy of an emerging new order impelling the effort. Leaders like Bresee and Maurice embodied its critical posture: here and now, in our neighborhood, on the reign and rule of God.

WORKS CITED

Allchin, A. M. *Participation in God: A Forgotten Strand in Anglican Tradition*. Wilton, CT: Morehouse-Barlow, 1988.

Bangs, Carl S. *Phineas F. Bresee: His Life in Methodism, the Holiness Movement and the Church of the Nazarene*. Kansas City, MO: Beacon Hill P, 1995.

Bassett, Paul M. "Prognosis: The Possibilities for Wesleyan Renewal." H. Orton Wiley Lecture Series: *Salutary Relapse: The Holiness Movement's Recovery of Her Roots*. Point Loma Nazarene College, 9 Feb. 1994.

Brauer, Jerald C., ed. *The Lively Experiment Continued*. Macon, GA: Mercer P, 1987.

Crocker, Chester A. *High Noon in Southern Africa: Making Peace in a Rough Neighborhood*. New York: Norton, 1993.

Dulles, Avery. *Models of the Church*. 1978. New York: Image-Doubleday, 1987.

Erwin, Gayle D. *The Jesus Style*. Dallas: Word, 1988.

Fowl, Stephen E. and L. Gregory Jones. *Reading in Communion: Scripture and Ethics.* Grand Rapids, MI: Eerdmans, 1991.

Gaybba, Brian. "Love, the Lamp of Theology." *Journal of Theology for Southern Africa.* 87 (1987):27-33.

Hauerwas, Stanley and William H. Willimon. *Resident Aliens: Life in the Christian Colony.* Nashville: Abingdon, 1989.

Hawthorne, John and David P. Whitelaw. "The Interface between Theology and Sociology: An Interdisciplinary Approach." Address. Society for the Scientific Study of Religion Conference. Virginia Beach, VA, 9 Nov. 1990.

Leffel, G. Michael. "From 'Barely' to 'Fully' Personal: On the Therapeutic Action of Prevenient Grace Within the Personality." *Grace in the Academic Community: Festschrift for Cecil R. Paul.* Ed. Maxine E. Walker. San Diego: Point Loma P, 1996. 115-131.

Loder, Ted. *Guerrillas of Grace: Prayers for the Battle.* San Diego: Luramedia, 1984.

Maurice, Frederick D. *The Lord's Prayer.* New York: Hurd and Houghton, 1872.

Mead, Sidney E. *The Lively Experiment: The Shaping of Christianity in America.* 1963 New York: Harper, 1976.

Nouwen, Henri. *Reaching Out: The Three Movements of the Spiritual Life.* 1975. New York: Image-Doubleday, 1986.

Oberman, Heiko A. *Luther: Man Between God and the Devil.* New Haven: Yale UP, 1989.

Pacini, David. "Excursus, Reading Holy Writ: The Locus of Modern Spirituality" *Christian Spirituality: Post-Reformation and Modern.* By Louis Dupre and Don E. Saliers. New York: Crossroad, 1991. 174-210.

Paoli, Arturo. *Gather Together in My Name: Reflections on Christianity and Community.* New York: Orbis, 1987.

Snyder, Howard A. *Models of the Kingdom.* Nashville: Abingdon, 1991.

Tracy, David. *The Analogical Imagination: Christian Theology and the Culture of Pluralism.* New York: Crossroad, 1981.

Van Beeck, Frans Joseph. *God Encountered: A Contemporary Catholic Systematic Theology.* Vol.1 of 3 vols. to date. San Francisco: Harper, 1989- .

Watson, David Lowes. *Forming Christian Disciples: The Role of Covenant Discipleship and Class Leaders in the Congregation.* Nashville: Discipleship Resources, 1991.

Winter, Ralph D. and R. Pierce Beaver. *The Warp and the Woof: Organizing for Mission.* Pasadena: William Carey Library, 1970.

Wuthnow, Robert. *Sharing the Journey: Support Groups and America's New Quest for Community.* New York: Macmillan/Free P, 1994.

Wynkoop, Mildred B. "Theological Roots of the Wesleyan Understanding of the Holy Spirit." *Wesleyan Theological Journal.* (1979): 77-98.

Zizioulas, John D. *Being As Communion.* New York: St. Vladimir's Seminary P, 1985.

Whitelaw, David, *Ph.D. Dr. Whitelaw is the Director of Graduate Studies in Religion at Point Loma Nazarene College. He is Professor of historical and practical theology in the Department of Philosophy and Religion and recently served as the department chair. Before coming to PLNC, he chaired the Division of Religion at Olivet Nazarene University. A native of South Africa, he served for eleven years as a pastor before being elected the District Superintendent of the Republic of South Africa European District.*

CHAPTER EIGHT

THE CHURCH OF THE NAZARENE: UNDERCURRENTS OF A CHANGING IDENTITY

Ron Benefiel

The persuasion that a particular theological perspective is uniquely
truth . . .
The unifying influence of a charismatic leader . . .
Shared life experiences of a social class, ethnicity, sacrifice or
persecution . . .
Common beliefs that manifest themselves in agreed upon common
norms . . .

These are just a few of the factors that often contribute to the formation
and development of the cultural core identity and value structure of a
religious group. Once this core identity is birthed, it seems to take on
something of a life of its own. It persists over time and has the capability of
engendering deep commitment among the faithful. It is central to the
"reason for being" of the group. It serves to give the members of the group
a sense of connectedness. But with the passing of time, diversification of
the group, and increased tolerance of divergent opinions, the core identity inevitably faces the pressures of change. The once uniting, commonly
held theologies, world views and prescriptive behaviors are challenged by
competing perspectives and questions about the relevance of particular
norms. The group is faced with the threatening prospect of the fragmentation of its core value structure.

The Church of the Nazarene has likely always been a more diverse
group than its collective conscience might recall. Many of the church's
beginnings were associated with revivalism and "brush arbors" in rural
nineteenth-century America, yet the leadership of Phineas Bresee
emerged out of the urban center of Los Angeles. The movement is often
historically associated with the lower social classes, and yet there were people of influence by any standard who were very active and prominent in its
beginnings. Its theological roots are usually traced back to Methodism, yet
many of those who came into the Church of the Nazarene in its beginnings were from a number of different denominational backgrounds.

Even so, perhaps like the amalgamation of a multitude of immigrants into an American nationalism, the Church of the Nazarene in America developed an identity that was strong and seemingly quite homogeneous. There was a strong sense of "we-ness" and a shared commitment to what "we" were about in the world. But with the passing of time there are indications that the strong sense of focused identity seems to be giving way to a variety of competing identities. It is the hypothesis of this chapter that this long-standing commitment to a commonly embraced set of Nazarene core values, norms and beliefs is undergoing a significant reorientation, perhaps even fragmentation. It is my purpose here to explore what characterizes people called "Nazarenes" today and whether or not there are multiple sets of world views and value orientations developing within the general membership of the church.

There are a number of underlying social forces that may be contributing to "behind-the-scenes" identity shifts in religious movements generally, which may be specifically operable in the Church of the Nazarene, including:

1. The upward socio-economic mobility of the membership moving it away from the zeal and solidarity that sectness provides toward a mainstream "respectable" identity;

2. The increased educational levels in the membership adding to the numbers of pastors and leaders who are trained to think critically and to question authority;

3. The resultant loss of a sectarian "shield" making the church more vulnerable to the competing influences of political, cultural, and theological values from other religious groups and society as a whole;

4. The socio-religious environment of society de-emphasizing the significance of denominational affiliation in favor of local identity;

5. The emergence of the establishment-wary "Boomers" and "X-ers" in leadership;

6. The continued trend toward urbanization forcing a church with rural roots to adapt to a changing society;

7. The effect of sheer size on an organization as it moves from a denomination of a half-million members toward a million and a half world wide.

Each of these factors and all of them together may contribute to a denominational cultural environment that is especially open to change and vulnerable to outside influences.

The Typology

In an effort to measure whether or not there is in fact a fragmentation of the church's identity, an ideal typology (theoretical model) was constructed suggesting six distinct identities, three sets of dyads. The first set of dyads, "traditional" (T) and "neo-fundamentalist" (NF), represent the conservative nature of the church. The traditional type consists of loyal, older, long-time Nazarenes of the lower middle socio-economic strata who live mostly in rural areas and smaller towns in the South and Midwest and who generally attend smaller churches. The typology calls for them to be true to the traditional terminology, programs, rules and culture of past Nazarenedom. The great mission of the church is evangelism and the propagation of holiness.

The partner identity in the dyad, neo-fundamentalist, is traditional in its focus, but draws heavily from outside influences like the Christian Coalition. This group consists of a broad spectrum of society drawing from all age groups, community sizes, and regions. The mission is to preserve "traditional moral and family values" leading its proponents to go public on issues of homosexuality, abortion, and prayer in schools. The call to reform is based on the strong belief that the world is an evil place and getting worse in a hurry. The rationale for engagement is to "preserve what we can of value in our society for the sake of our children."

The second dyad is also influenced from outside the church, drawing especially from other evangelical groups whose theologies and methods are meeting with apparent success in the market place. The first of these, charismatic (Ch), is characterized by an emphasis on the power theologies and praise-oriented worship styles typical of Pentecostal churches. Nazarene identity and loyalty are much less defined than in the previous types and play a secondary role to the religious identity of the member, which is local in its orientation. The mission of the church is to worship God, and through spiritual gifts, accept the church's God-given authority over distress, disease and the "spiritual forces of darkness."

The second type in this dyad is contemporary (Co). This group is especially committed to expressing the gospel in ways that relate to the needs and everyday issues of people in American society. Its constituency tends to be younger and suburban and its approach is upbeat and drawing. Tradition is shelved in favor of relevance. Growth may be rapid, although sometimes unrooted. Awareness of Nazarene identity is secondary and distant.

The third dyad finds its identity in the traditions, symbols and spirit of historical Christianity. Those in this dyad are liberal in the sense of embracing winds of change in the church yet traditional in the sense that what is embraced is a rediscovery of the broader traditions within historical Christianity. The first type in this dyad is neo-Wesleyan or social concern (SC). Its constituency is mostly young adult, higher educated, urban members who have grown up in the church and whose loyalty to the church is stronger than their identification with the church as it currently presents itself. The mission of the church is wholistic with a commitment to both the personal and social dimensions of the gospel. Evil in the world is understood not only in terms of personal immorality, but also in terms of social injustice.

The final type, neo-evangelical (NE), is of negligible size and influence in the church at this point, but may be one of the emerging identities of the future. It is post-denominational in its orientation, relating more to the historical creedal symbols of the Church of Jesus Christ than specifically to the Church of the Nazarene. It is especially characterized by its ecumenical spirit and liturgical worship.

Methodology

A questionnaire was constructed for the purpose of testing the typology. Respondents were asked to order six possible responses (each representing one of the six types) in two questions, the sum of responses of which identified each respondent's typology profile. All respondents ranking highly the indicated items for a given type were considered to be representative of that type. Additional items were included to get a sense of how members of different types viewed denominational loyalty, political world view, and the perceived mission of the church.

The questionnaire was distributed to the panel of respondents in the Answer Poll, a randomly selected sample taken from membership lists of randomly selected churches clustered for church size and region in the United States and Canada. Survey responses were also collected from pastors but not utilized for the purposes of this study. Two hundred eleven responses were received and processed which represents a return rate of 40.5%.

Results and Data Analysis

The profile of the sample revealed a population that is female, middle-aged, middle socio-economic status, loyal to denominational affiliation, and politically conservative.

Gender: An unexpectedly high percent of the sample is female (63%). Unless there is a reporting bias favoring women, this would indicate a significant imbalance between men and women in the local congregation.

Age: The median age of respondents was 54 with the mean figuring in at 53. The average number of years that respondents reported being "Nazarene" was 26.5 (the median was 24). Again, unless there is a selection or reporting bias, this would indicate a very high percentage of members being elderly and long-term members of the church.

Socio-economic Level : The median level of education was high school graduate with some college or vocational school training. Forty-one percent were college graduates with eighteen percent earning graduate degrees. Thirty percent reported having attended a Nazarene college. The three most frequently checked occupations out of a list of 14 possibilities were professional (27%), clerk (17%) and executive (14%). The average reported household income was about $40,000 per year with 20% earning less than $25,000 and 10% earning more than $75,000 per year. These figures, by most standards, place the membership squarely in the middle class.

Denominational Loyalty: Even with evidence of changes taking place in the core identity of the Church, denominational loyalty remains quite strong. Forty-two percent of respondents said they cannot imagine a time when they will not be Nazarene. Another 43% said they were committed to the Church but might attend a church in another holiness or evangelical denomination someday. Only 6 percent indicated they did not really think of themselves as Nazarene with 9% replying that though they were Nazarene now they could "easily" see themselves attending a church in another denomination.

Political Preference: In the survey sample, 8% of respondents were Democrats, 74% were Republicans, 13% were independent, and 5% other (including responses from Canada). Given that Republicans and political independents tend toward conservative political positions and that a share of the Nazarene Democrat pool is likely to be conservative Southern Democrat, the political makeup of the church appears to be overwhelmingly, and nearly universally, conservative.

The political world views of respondents were further explored with inquiries about their opinions on various social programs and political figures (VF=Very Favorable, F=Favorable, U=Unfavorable, VU=Very Unfavorable and DK=Don't Know):

	VF%	F%	U%	VU%	DK%
HUD	2.5	21.5	28.5	13.0	34.5
Food Stamps	1.0	25.2	42.2	16.0	15.5
Affirmative Action	1.5	13.0	32.5	29.5	23.5
Planned Parenthood	7.3	13.2	18.5	48.3	12.7

Focus on the Family	66.0	29.7	0.5	—	3.8
Christian Coalition	15.3	42.6	9.9	5.4	26.7
Rush Limbaugh	13.9	39.1	17.3	10.9	18.8

These figures further confirm the politically conservative disposition of the church's membership. One would expect that this would have a corresponding impact on the membership's perspective on the kinds of social issues the church should engage (i.e., abortion, prayer in schools, etc.). In fact, when asked if they would feel more comfortable in a church advocating traditional values or in a church that was an agent of social change, 90% said they would prefer the church advocating traditional values. Nevertheless, there is a significant feeling that the church should be involved in responding to social problems and the needs of the poor. (For the following questions, SA=Strongly Agree, A=Agree, D=Disagree, SD=Strongly Disagree, and U=Unsure.)

The Church can and should make a significant difference in the social conditions of the world (i.e., poverty, hunger, homelessness, race relations).

SA%	A%	D%	SD%	U%
45.2	48.1	4.3	0.5	1.9

I think the church should actively take a stand against abortion.

62.7	29.2	6.2	0.5	1.4

I think the church should actively support prayer in public schools.

48.8	38.6	8.2	3.4	1.0

I think the church should actively work to eliminate poverty in the world.

13.5	59.4	18.4	2.4	6.3

I think the church should be actively involved in the effort to reduce crime in the community.

22.0	58.0	13.2	1.0	5.9

With respect to an overall perception of the "world", the responses are varied and somewhat complex. Sixty percent responded that they would feel more comfortable in a church that is "a kingdom presence" in a hurting world compared to 40% who favored being part of a church that was characterized as a word of truth to a hostile world. But 70% responded that the contemporary culture is mostly evil and 90% agreed or strongly agreed that the world is getting worse. Ninety-nine and one-half percent agreed that the only hope for the world is spiritual revival.

In conceptualizing evil, 78% often or very often thought of evil in terms of Satanic power and spiritual warfare and 95% in terms of immorality and personal responsibility compared to only 49% who thought in terms of systemic evil and social justice.

The questionnaire also included some questions that could be viewed as indicators of tolerance/intolerance. If a critique of conservative political positions has often been in the arena of tolerance (racial separation, women's issues, etc.) and if the tradition in the Christian community is one of tolerance, how are these competing values integrated by members of a politically conservative church? The respondents were asked their opinion on the following items (VF=Very Favorable, F=Favorable, U=Unfavorable, VU=Very Unfavorable and DK=Don't Know):

	VF%	F%	U%	VU%	DK%
Exporting Illegal Immigrants	16.5	46.6	15.5	3.9	17.5
Roman Catholic Church	0.5	37.3	33.3	7.8	21.6

I would welcome a woman as senior pastor of our congregation. (A=Agree, D=Disagree)

SA%	A%	D%	SD%	Unsure%
9.0	29.0	25.2	8.1	28.6

Even though various rationale may be put forth in support of different positions (e.g., illegal immigrants should be exported because they are in violation of the law), these responses represent a degree of intolerance among the church membership. This is especially poignant when it comes to women in ministry as this is specifically stated as a value the church formally embraces.

Testing the Typology

Several challenges were encountered in analyzing the data, especially when it came to the matter of testing the typology. Small numbers of respondents were anticipated for all but the Traditional (T) and Neo-Fundamentalist (NF) types. This proved to be especially true for the Social Concern (SC) and Neo-Evangelical (NE) types with only 6 and 7 respondents being placed in each respective type. The small number in these types prevented any kind of substantive analysis in relation to other variables.

	T	NF	Ch	Co	SC	NE
%	43	50	45	16	3	4
N	85	98	89	32	6	7

(Note: The total adds to more than 100 % because some respondents were high in more than one type.)

Secondly, when comparing the four types which do have enough respondents for further data analysis, there is very little variance in frequency distributions between types on most items in the survey. Some of this may be explained by the fact that the sample is relatively homogeneous with regard to such variables as denominational loyalty and political preference.

If there is little variance on many questions, and if some types have negligible numbers, then we must conclude that the typology does not identify discrete cohorts within the sample, at least not around the variables being tested. Our conclusion based on the data analysis to this point would be that there remains a strong rather homogeneous unifying core identity and culture in the church that can be understood not only in terms of theological distinctive but also in terms of political world view. However, additional statistical analysis reveals a more complicated picture.

Enter factor analysis. Factor analysis gives us the ability to understand tendencies within the sample as a whole that do not necessarily show up when dividing the sample into discrete types by analyzing which responses to various questions tend to cluster together. A factor is formed when those who respond in one direction on a given question are likely to respond in a similar direction on other questions. Due to the limited capacity of the statistics program, questions on the survey were divided into two parts for the purpose of analysis.

In submitting the data to factor analysis, a number of factors were produced, the following seven of which appear to be most helpful in understanding trends and tendencies within the population. Responses to items in the questionnaire which we might have expected to hang together in line with the typology, did so. For example, the following sets of responses clustered together and were loaded on the corresponding factors (factor coefficients are noted in parentheses):

Factor #1

(.818) I would only consider Nazarene churches in my search for a new church home.
(.767) I cannot imagine a time when I will not be a Nazarene.
(.547) V.H. Lewis, Stephen Manley, Chuck Milhuff
(.507) Sanctification is the distinct work of the Holy Spirit in the life of the believer in which the old sinful nature is eradicated...

Factor #2

(.654) I think the church should actively support prayer in public schools.
(.652) Sin is always a clear issue of right and wrong.
(.625) The world is getting worse.

(.489) I think the church should actively take a stand against abortion.

Factor #3

(–.701) Better understanding of the life issues of people who live in the community so that the church can be relevant in addressing the needs of people in a changing world.

(.650) Getting people saved through organized personal evangelism and evangelistic revival campaigns.

(–.459) Developing "compassionate ministry centers" and advocating for the rights of the poor.

Factor #4

(.666) Worship services in which the poor are welcomed, and preaching that emphasizes social justice, racial reconciliation, and compassion for the downtrodden.

(.556) I am probably most comfortable in a church that is an agent of social change in the community. (compared to one which is an advocate for traditional values).

(.539) When I think about evil in our world, I usually think in terms of systemic evil and social justice.

Factor #5

(.859) favorable opinion about Nazarene Headquarters

(.851) favorable opinion about Nazarene Publishing House

(.838) favorable opinion about Nazarene Bible College

(.797) favorable opinion about Nazarene Theological Seminary

(.701) favorable opinion about Nazarene Compassionate Ministries

(.608) favorable opinion about *Herald of Holiness*

Factor #6

(.786) favorable opinion about Fuller Theological Seminary

(.670) favorable opinion about *Christianity Today*

(.616) favorable opinion about Asbury Theological Seminary

(.539) favorable opinion about *Grow* magazine

(.454) favorable opinion about World Vision

Factor #7

(.758) favorable opinion about Rush Limbaugh

(.728) favorable opinion about exporting illegal immigrants

(.621) favorable opinion about the Christian Coalition

(.488) favorable opinion about the Roman Catholic Church

(.465) favorable opinion about the National Council of Churches

Each of the factors appears to have some rationale linking the responses together (with the noted exception of the last two items in factor #7). In each of the cases, the rationale can be understood to be more or less linked to one of the types in our typological model. Factors #1 and #5 appear to line up with the Traditional type, factors #2 and #7 with the Neo-Fundamentalist type, factor #6 with the Neo-Evangelical type, and factor #4 with the Social Concern type. Factor #3, while suggesting the possibility of a relationship between values portrayed by the Social Concern and Contemporary types distances each from the value of traditional forms of evangelism (characteristic of the Traditional type). Again, while organized cohorts are not necessarily being identified, these factors strongly suggest that there are different configurations of core values and orientations embraced within the population.[1]

Conclusion

The Church of the Nazarene has experienced a long period of internal solidarity, corporate identity and commonly shared core values. Our hunch that all this may be changing is difficult to measure past the normative changes in rules and standards and the programmatic changes in Sunday School contests and youth meetings. This research effort has been an attempt to define and measure the splintering of the church's core identity and value complex. The data failed to identify discrete cohort groups around different value orientations or types. Instead, the population presented itself as a rather homogeneous group, particularly in regard to political world view, with a persistent denominational loyalty.

However, upon further analysis of the data, hints of cross-currents within the flow of the stream of members were detected. The fragmentation of identity is not yet measured by organized groups with competing agendas, but rather by the confusing and conflicting values which promise to become more prominent in the future. If the church is left without a strong core identity and shared value system, it follows that it will become increasingly vulnerable to adopting popular theologies and values from outside groups and the mainstream of society.

The implications for pastors are especially significant. Increasingly, pastors may be surprised by the emergence of new and disparate theological identities in churches they might have considered to have been strongly traditional "Nazarene" in orientation. Furthermore, they may discover that some congregations are defined more by political world view than by theological conviction or heritage.

Primary Theological/Sub-Cultural Identities in the
North American Church of the Nazarene

1) Traditional

constituency:	age - 50+ ; SES - lower/lower-middle Region -especially Mid-West and South Generation/tenure Nazarene - long, third generation+; church size - mostly smaller community size - mostly rural
world view:	localistic/dualistic
view of the church:	lighthouse, family, internal focus, ministry occurs inside the church
mission of the church:	to persevere as the holy remnant
attitude toward the world:	evil, lost, a field of evangelism
programs:	Sunday School, Prayer meeting, revivals, camp meetings, traditional worship, VBS, NWMS societies
theological and cultural values:	individualism, politically conservative, eradication view of holiness, evangelism, separation from the world reinforced by rules, anti-Pentecostal
spirit:	isolationist, conservative, sometimes reactionary
Nazarene identity:	strong with great loyalty, will always be Nazarene and attend Nazarene church
% of Nazarene churches:	25
% of Nazarenes:	10

2) Neo-Fundamentalist

constituency:	all ages, all regions, all generations Nazarene, all church sizes SES - lower middle and middle community context - suburban/rural
world view:	localistic, dualistic
view of the church:	conservator of religious and cultural values, church takes prophetic/activist role in community on issues relating to personal morality and religious freedom (i.e. communism, homosexuality, abortion, prayer in schools)
mission of the church:	preserve traditional moral and family values

attitude toward the world:	world is evil, getting worse, threatening all we value and hold to be true
programs:	modified traditional, mostly traditional worship, ministry is primarily within the church, in the community primarily known for what it is against, protests change in society (especially moral change).
theological and cultural values:	individualism, God and country, family, politically
conservative spirit:	angry, control-withdrawal
prophets:	Jerry Falwell, James Dobson, Pat Robertson
Nazarene Identity:	fairly strong Nazarene identity whether or not attending a Nazarene church in the future
% of Nazarene churches:	60
% of Nazarenes:	65

3) Charismatic

constituency:	age - all ages but especially young adult tenure Nazarene — short, first generation church size - growing; SES - middle community context - suburban
world view:	dualistic (enemy is Satan), localistic
view of the church:	worship center
mission of the church:	worship and spiritual warfare
attitude toward the world:	aggressive, entrepreneurial
programs:	contemporary/charismatic worship, small groups, emphasis on healing, spiritual gifts, spiritual warfare
theological and cultural values:	?
spirit:	upbeat, drawing, but often divisive
prophets:	Jack Hayford, John Wimber
Nazarene identity:	very weak, fairly independent in nature
% of Nazarene churches:	5
% of Nazarenes:	15

4) Contemporary

constituency:	age — young adult; tenure Nazarene — full range, many newcomers church size — full range, mostly middle to large community context — suburban; SES — middle
world view:	cosmopolitan, shades of gray
view of the church:	center of seeker-sensitive evangelism, worship center
mission of the church:	new definitions of old mission based on relevance to society
attitude toward the world:	interesting, hurting
programs:	praise oriented worship, small groups, church growth
theological and cultural values:	go with what works, relevance, progressive redefinitions of theological language and missiological form
spirit:	risk-taking, energetic, progressive
prophets:	Bill Hybels, John Maxwell
Nazarene identity:	fairly weak
% of Nazarene churches:	5
% of Nazarenes:	5

5) Neo-Wesleyan / Social Concern

constituency:	age - young adult tenure Nazarene - long term Nazarene church size - small to mid-size community context - urban SES - leaders are middle (high education)/constituency is poor
world view:	shades of gray, cosmopolitan, wholistic
view of the church:	community in mission
mission of the church:	social transformation within an evangelical framework
attitude toward the world:	dominated by systemic injustice
programs:	community-based "compassionate ministries," worship varies from liturgical to contemporary

theological and cultural values:	incarnational approach to ministry, politically moderate to liberal, emphasis on personal "spirituality" and social dimensions of the Gospel, activism centers on issues of social justice (poverty, racial discrimination, etc.) from a wholistic perspective
spirit:	tolerant, risk-taking, weary, progressive
prophets:	Tom Nees, Tony Campolo, Ron Sider, Jim Wallis
Nazarene identity:	stronger on personal loyalty than on denominational identity, ecumenical spirit
% of Nazarene churches:	5
% of Nazarenes:	5

6) Neo-Evangelical

constituency:	young adult to middle aged, higher education and SES especially in and around college communities; tenure Nazarene — long term, second or third generation
world view:	cosmopolitan, shades of gray
view of the church:	local parish, worshipping community
mission of the church:	to be the faithful witness of the historical creedal Church in and to the world
attitude toward the world:	neutral
programs:	liturgical worship, social awareness regarding issues of social justice and the environment
theological and cultural values:	politically moderate to liberal, emphasis on spirituality in the context of community, open theological thought
spirit:	pensive, contemplative, reverent, both evangelical and ecumenical
prophets:	Lloyd Ogilvie
% of Nazarene churches:	negligible, just dawning
% of Nazarene members:	negligible, either have left the church for mainline denomination or are participating in both Nazarene and main-line churches

NOTE

1. This is further supported in examining correlation coefficients between the factors (probabilities are listed below correlation coefficients in parentheses):

	1	2	3	4	5	6	7
factor #1	1.00	.031	.133	-.087	.481	.032	-.077
		(.71)	(.11)	(.35)	(.000)	(.71)	(.37)
factor #2		1.00	.238	-.029	.199	.058	.256
			(.001)	(.72)	(.005)	(.44)	(.000)
factor #3			1.00	-.090	.168	.083	.159
				(.26)	(.02)	(.27)	(.03)
factor #4				1.00	.128	.275	.039
					(.11)	(.001)	(.63)
factor #5					1.00	.392	.079
						(.000)	(.28)
factor #6						1.00	.131
							(.08)
factor #7							1.00

Several factors are highly correlated in line with our expectations as they describe the same type or correlations of dyads in our model. For example, the responses in the items in the Traditional factors #1 and #5 are highly correlated as are the items in the Neo-Fundamentalist factors, #2 and #7 . The correlations between #2 and #3 and between #2 and #5 suggest a bridge between the two types (high correlations between factors representing dyad pairs in the model). Further the correlation of the items in #4 with those in #6 suggest a bridge between Social Concern and Neo-Evangelical values.

It is also of interest to note the factors that are not correlated with each other. The items in Traditional factor #1 are not correlated with Neo-Evangelical #6 and are negatively related to Social Concern #4 as the typological model would predict. However, #1 is also not correlated with Neo-Fundamentalist factors #2 or #7, suggesting a distinct separation in the population between some Traditional and Neo-Fundamentalist values. Neo-Fundamentalist factor #2 is not correlated with Social Concern #4 or Neo-Evangelical #6. The lack of correlations between factors #3 and #4 and between #4 and #7 are also in line with what the model would predict.

WORKS CITED

Bainbridge, William Sims and Rodney Stark. "Sectarian Tension." *Review of Religious Research* 22.2 (1980):105-124.

Bangs, Carl. *Phineas F. Bresee: His Life in Methodism, the Holiness Movement, and the Church of the Nazarene.* Kansas City, MO: Beacon Hill P, 1995.

Bibby, Reginald W. "Why Conservative Churches Really Are Growing: Kelley Revisited." *Journal for the Scientific Study of Religion* 17.2 (1978):129-137.

Iannaccone, Laurence R. "Why Strict Churches Are Strong." *American Journal of Sociology* 99.5 (1994): 1180-1211.

Johnson, Benton. "On Church and Sect." *American Sociological Review* 28.4 (1963):539-549.

Kelley, Dean M. *Why Conservative Churches Are Growing.* New York: Harper, 1972.

McGuire, Meredith B. *Religion: The Social Context.* Belmont, CA: Wadsworth, 1981.

Mead, Loren B. *The Once and Future Church.* 1991. Washington: Alban Institute Publication, 1994.

Niebuhr, H. Richard. *The Social Sources of Denominationalism.* New York: Meridian, 1929.

Wilson, Bryan R. *Patterns of Sectarianism: Organization and Ideology in Social and Religious Movements.* London: Heinemann, 1967.

Wuthnow, Robert. *Christianity in the 21st Century.* New York: Oxford UP, 1993.

Benefiel, Ron, Ph.D. Dr. Benefiel currently teaches urban ministry and sociology courses at Point Loma Nazarene College, after having served as Associate or Senior Pastor of Los Angeles First Church of the Nazarene for 20 years. Benefiel has conducted extensive study about the impact of cultural trends on the traditions and membership make-up of the Church of the Nazarene. While pastoring, he also directed the Bresee Foundation, which offers health, food, and employment services to the homeless of downtown Los Angeles.

CHAPTER NINE

INCARNATIONAL MINISTRY: WHO IN THE WORLD DO YOU THINK YOU ARE?

Norm Shoemaker

The title given to this chapter is more than an attempt to be clever. It is not just a play on words. This question—Who in the world do you think you are?—probes the heart of vocational identity in ministry. In a recent conversation with a pastor friend he remarked, "I think I'm having an identity crisis." He was not regressing to adolescence or living through a second round of puberty. Even as a mature Christian leader, this friend was struggling with the "models" of ministry presented by the contemporary culture as it stands on the threshold of a new millennium. He continued to pour out his obvious frustration, "Am I supposed to be a Village Chaplain? Corporate CEO? Church Growth Guru? Servant Leader? As a minister, who in the world am I?"

Modern media is quick to offer a response. Television and the movies often characterize the Christian pastor as everything from a patronizing buffoon to a "hip dude" on a Harley known as "The Rev." But seldom is she portrayed as a faithful servant of God. However, if pastoral identity today sports a black eye, in many respects, it is self-inflicted. The highly publicized scandals of recent years involving high profile pastors have not only resulted in their personal "fall from grace" but have further eroded respect and trust for people in vocational ministry. In an environment of mistrust and confusion from both within and without the church, the question continues to emerge: Christian minister . . . who in the world are you? In the midst of such diverse "models" for ministry, is there a "map" that might guide a serious, although brief, reflection on the essential nature of pastoral vocation?

A Theological Focus

What is the defining center for an appropriate understanding of ministry? What is that "center core" that informs the pastoral vocation? Is it the culture? Personal needs? Church tradition? Congregational expectations? Consumer surveys?

Think about it! What if an understanding of the pastor's identity and role was shaped by an incarnational model? And, what if out of that model, we developed a "map" for ministry? What if, as Thomas Oden suggests, we allowed our ecclesiology to follow our Christology (57)? Let us review a few "snapshots" from the Gospels.

When considering an incarnational model for ministry, the passage that immediately comes to mind is the defining prologue to the Gospel of John. First, "In the beginning was the Word, and the Word was with God, and the Word was God. He was with God in the beginning" (1:1-2) . And then John continues, "The Word became flesh and made his dwelling place among us" (1:14a).

Clearly, Scripture and creed not only affirm that Jesus is God of God, Light of Light, very God of very God, but also bone of our bone and flesh of our flesh. For the sake of men and women and "for . . . our salvation [He] came down from heaven, and was incarnate by the Holy Spirit. . . " (Nicene Creed). Volumes upon volumes have been written explicating this essential mystery of the historic Faith. Risking severe over-simplification, let it be said that the Christian tradition affirms that there is no "ellipsis" between Jesus and the Father-God and that there is no "ellipsis" between Jesus and humankind. From this historic affirmation there are at least three thematic implications that appear relevant.

First, an incarnational model exists with *dynamic tension*. In an introductory course on systematic theology a student learns that these two aspects of Christ's nature—the divine and the human—exist in dynamic tension. Most, if not all, of the Christological heresies grow out of an attempt to "soften" or reduce this paradoxical tension. Reducing the logical tension effects a Christological distortion. Likewise, a distorted incarnational model will profoundly affect the fundamental character and expression of ministry. In other words, the "model" may ultimately become the "map" that guides and defines ministry. Incarnational models shape the way people "do" ministry.

In the very practical day-to-day work of ministry, a pastor faces and experiences this dynamic tension. For example, take a "high and holy calling" and place it in the context of a very real, fallen world, and what do you have? Tension! Most "real world" people have little appreciation for a "holy calling." Yet, a pastor in contextualizing ministry is called to do "real ministry" in a "real world." Sometimes, in an attempt to relate to people, a pastor can be tempted to *devalue* the notion of a "holy calling." When this occurs, ministry suffers from reductionism. The pastoral birthright is subtly *sold* or exchanged for the common porridge of *consumer satisfaction* and *market friendly* affirmations. The "holy calling" is reduced to something more akin to . . . a relational therapist . . . political advocate . . . moral mentor . . . or personal growth guide. Reductionism distorts incarnational ministry to its fleshly side (Oden 55).

On the other hand, when we obscure the very human side of ministry in a real world, then ministry is seen as "above and beyond" the needs of people; something foreign to "life here and now." Thus, ministry is perceived as detached . . . irrelevant . . . and other-worldly. Thomas Oden has his finger on the pulse of the issue when in his text on *Pastoral Theology: Essentials of Ministry* he writes, "When the divine and human sides are held together, ministry can be seen more wholly as human response to divine gift, a beautiful amalgam of graced nature and naturally embodied grace" (55). When we reduce "pastor" to just a *friend, promoter, guide, activist,* then we affirm Christian ministry to be very human but not very divine. On the other hand, if we profile the pastoral role as a "high and holy" position, living above and beyond it all, then we affirm ministry as divine but certainly not "like me." Either way, ministry is distorted by an improper Christological tension.

The second guiding theme to be drawn from an incarnational model of pastoral ministry is the *significance of presence.* In the Gospel of Matthew the writer "connects" with the prophetic words of Isaiah and presents Jesus as Immanuel. "The virgin will be with child and will give birth to a son, and they will call him Immanuel—which means, 'God with us'" (1:23). This is truly astounding. God in Christ has entered into the stream of our own human existence to fully share our life. This, in and of itself, is good news. An incarnational model reminds ministers-in-the-making that presence or being precedes doing. The fact that God has come to "be" with us makes this world a different place. Presence does not have to "do something" in order to be significant.

In offering the "sacrament of presence" and in practicing the art of "showing up," a person in ministry can also make a difference. Henri Nouwen is a contemporary "care-giver" who deeply understands the gift of caring presence. In his book *Compassion,* Nouwen writes,

> In a time so filled with methods and techniques designed to change people, to influence their behavior, and to make them do new things and think new thoughts, we have lost the simple but difficult gift of being present to each other. We have lost this gift because we have been led to believe that presence must be useful. (14)

Through the Incarnation we make the freeing discovery that God's ultimate gift is the gift of Himself.

Finally, ministry defined by an incarnational model is characterized by *radical identification.* Through the Incarnation we are reminded that "the One who has been there" is "the One who is here . . . with me." In Christ, we have One who really does understand. The writer to the Hebrews says, "For we do not have a high priest who is unable to sympathize with our weaknesses, but we have one who has been tempted in every way, just as we are—yet was without sin. Let us then approach the throne of grace with confidence " (4:15-16a). Jesus' coming to us enables us to come to him. He put on our flesh. He walked in our shoes. He lived in our skin. He faced what we face and more. He has embraced everything human with the infinite tenderness of grace.

A Biblical Lens

We come back to the central question: *Who in the world do you think you are?* How we answer is significant. This question probes the very heart, source and substance of our calling to ministry. The answer carves out our identity. It establishes our authenticity. It empowers our courage. It defines our very being.

If we must seek the answer to identity issues through the affirmation and approval of other people, then we can expect to be tempted by the allure of what "they" have to offer us—status, power, honor, recognition. As a result, we feel pushed to compete and compare our "ministries" in order to know how we are doing. This creates the illusion of status by pecking order (Manning 51). We are tempted to settle for the false security offered by "pleasing the right people." How does the person in ministry avoid being "jerked" around by the needs, agendas, expectations and dependencies of other people, yet remain free to love them and serve them in character-building ways? What if we allowed ministry to be defined by Jesus' calling? What if we believed that His calling was the defining center for "our call" to ministry? For a moment let us step back in time into Jesus' sandals and attempt to understand the nature of His call to servanthood.

The morning came. It was time. Jesus washed his face for the last time at home. He left his room, looked around, then closed the door. He embraced his mother, who followed him to the door. There was no turning back. He went to the nearest corner. Which way would he go? Matthew in a few brief words provides the answer, "Then Jesus came from Galilee to the Jordan to be baptized by John" (3:13). Can you believe it? The Incarnate Son of God stands in line just waiting for his turn to be baptized in the muddy Jordan River. As soon as Jesus was baptized, he went up out of the water. At that moment heaven was opened, and he saw the Spirit of God descending like a dove and lighting on him. And a voice from heaven said, "This is my Son, whom I love; with him I am well pleased" (Matt. 3:16-17).

In a brief and simple phrase, the core values of Jesus' identity and mission are affirmed and confirmed. In fact, Matthew makes it clear—this announcement must be heard and understood. It is strategic. Neither angels, prophets, nor divine messengers will be entrusted with this word. God will speak for himself. What does God say?

First, "This is my Son, whom I love" which echoes Psalm 2:7 identifying Jesus with the Messianic traditions. Who in the world is Jesus? The Father makes it undeniably clear: "You are my beloved Son." The second half of the Father's affirmation—"with him I am well pleased"—resonates with the suffering servant passages of Isaiah. Jesus is being called to servanthood. His "kingdom" will come not by raw power imposed on others against their will but by the gracious strength of sacrificial, self-giving love.

The essential mandate—*the call*—is clear. Jesus is to live out of the *love* of His Father. His calling is our calling in ministry. Let us be honest. It is easy to live out of other sources for affirmation and significance. We are easily tempted to live out of achievement, success, competition, self-focused priorities that promise praise from others. Jesus leaned into the love of His Father. Henri Nouwen states the issue plainly, "Jesus didn't have to prove to the world that he was worthy of love. He already was the 'Beloved,' and this Belovedness allowed him to live free from the manipulative games of the world, always faithful to the voice that had spoken to him at the Jordan" (*Here* 135-136).

Mark it down and count on it—anything essential to health and hope in ministry will be tested. We should not be surprised that the same Spirit that descended on Jesus in the Jordan led him "into the desert to be tempted by the devil" (Matthew 4:1). In the wilderness experience the enemy of authentic ministry zeroes in on the core values for ministry.

Tempted to turn rocks into bread, leap like a superstar from the temple roof and bow down to the fallen kingdoms of this world, Jesus resists by declaring and obeying his call to "sonship" and "servanthood." One can almost hear and feel the voice of attack: "Who in the world do you think you are?" The answer heard throughout the cosmos was and is, "I am the beloved of the Father." The Father's affirmation formed the core value which nurtured and sustained our Lord. It was not just a nice idea, an inspiring thought, but the defining word. Who in the world do you think you are? That is a good question. What is your answer?

Ministers are called to "live out" the love of God in concrete ways. Does an incarnational "model" provide a practical "map" for ministry? In other words, how is incarnational ministry "incarnated" in me, as a minister or a pastor?

A Personal Snapshot

Incarnational ministry jumped out of a textbook into the middle of my life on a typical Monday morning, following a better-than-typical Sunday, as the phone rang in my office. It was my son Steve. The tears ran down the phone line and into my heart. "Dad, can you come? Our baby has just died." I was no longer a professional pastor. I just prayed that I would be a competent father.

As I drove into the parking lot adjacent to the doctor's clinic, Steve and Janae, his wife, were waiting beside their car, holding each other in a soul-comforting embrace. I joined them in a group hug, our tears co-mingling on the asphalt below.

The next day, Janae, six months along in her pregnancy was admitted to the Mary Birch Birthing Center. As chemicals induced labor, we waited as Janae gave birth to death. In the room that Tuesday a pain-embracing, heart-breaking, three-letter word was screamed in silence—"Why...why?" That evening, little, lifeless Kayla was born. To watch your twenty-eight year-old son hold in his arms "all that might have been but never will be" is so incredibly painful. Parents feel called to help. But at such times, it is clear, there is nothing you can do. It hurts. Pure and simple.

A week later, I was scheduled to speak for a Good Friday Community Service at the Point Loma United Methodist Church. Various pastors from area churches were asked to speak on a "word" from the Cross. I was prepared to speak on the Sixth Word from the Cross— "It is finished" (John 19:30)! Two minutes before processing onto the platform, someone handed me an Order of Service. There was a mix-up. The bulletin listed my name beside the Fourth Word— "My God, my God, why have you forsaken me" (Matt. 27:46)?

I cannot recall the hymns we sang or what anybody else said during the ten minutes before I stepped up to the podium to speak. I was trying to "prepare" a new message on a different word. It finally dawned on me. The events of the past week in little Kayla's death had already prepared me. Stepping forward to address the worshippers, I related the events of the week, reliving what a Father feels when a beloved son hurts.

Following the "Amen" of the benediction, I lingered in the foyer of the church. A young lady approached, staring at the ground she whispered, "How many pounds was she?"

"Excuse me," I said not understanding the question.

"How many pounds was she? The baby?"

"Oh, I'm with you now," I replied. "I think she was about two and a half pounds."

"Mine was three pounds," she said through choked-back tears.

We embraced each other and cried. Together we took another step towards wholeness.

From that day to now, I have been thinking . . . when it comes to ministry? The "model" really is the "map."

WORKS CITED

The Bible. New International Version.

Manning, Brennan. *Abba's Child: The Cry of the Heart for Intimate Belonging.* Colorado Springs: Navpress, 1994.

Nouwen, Henri. *Here and Now.* New York: Crossroad, 1994.

——, Donald P. McNeill and Douglas A. Morrison. *Compassion: A Reflection on the Christian Life.* New York: Doubleday, 1982.

Oden, Thomas C. *Pastoral Theology: Essentials of Ministry.* San Francisco: Harper, 1983.

Shoemaker, Norm, *M.R.E. Rev. Shoemaker is Senior Pastor at San Diego First Church of the Nazarene. He served as the Director of Spiritual Development at Point Loma Nazarene College for eight years, coordinating campus ministry programs and providing leadership in the area of spiritual formation at the college. Before coming to San Diego, he pastored two churches and was General Program Director of Youth Ministries for the Nazarene denomination. He has written several books as well as numerous magazine articles on church ministry.*

CHAPTER TEN

PARTNERS IN MINISTRY: MEN AND WOMEN SERVING/ LEADING TOGETHER

Janine T. Metcalf

It came totally unexpected.

After the congregation prayed and sang a medley of praise choruses and hymns, I stepped up to the pulpit prepared to preach the morning's message. The joyous privilege to teach from God's Word was enhanced by an extraordinary awareness of divine presence. Every element of worship had poised us for a wonderful encounter with God. That's why the next few moments took us all by surprise.

A man in the middle of the congregation stood up, shook his finger at me and shouted, "No! You shouldn't be there!" He then stomped out and slammed the doors of the sanctuary behind him. All eyes followed him, then they reeled back to me.

Frankly, I had no answer for the man. God, however, enabled me to begin preaching with unusual ease, as if the incident had never occurred.

That morning was the first of many discouraging experiences I have endured while trying to heed God's call to preach. While the natural tendency would be to whine and feel sorry for myself, I can testify that God's grace has been sufficient to overcome any lingering resentment. After all, many women throughout the history of Christianity have faced similar discrimination.

The question that emerges is *why*? Why have women achieved equality and relative parity with men in most areas of society, except in the church? Why have women been able to distinguish themselves as educators, authors, artists, and administrators and been denied opportunities to use their gifts in the Body of Christ? The church is the community in which Christ's love and freedom should be modeled and embraced, not inhibited. Some of the key reasons for this disparity include:

1. *Disagreement over the controversial passages of Paul that would seem to prohibit women from speaking and leading in the church* (1 Cor. 14:34-35; 1 Tim. 2:11-15): Certain conservative evangelical leaders contend these passages clearly affirm the principle of male-head-ship in the home and church. However, before issuing a blanket prohibition against women

preaching and leading in ministry, the church should take a closer look at the historical context of these passages. Did Paul intend to generally limit ministry roles available to women, or was he addressing specific problems that most likely existed in Corinth and Ephesus? Do these verses support or contradict an overall tenure of Scripture that encourages every believer to use his or her spiritual gifts to help build the Body of Christ?

2. *Discrimination against women throughout history:* Male dominance and female subordination have characterized most cultures since the dawn of recorded history. Until the twentieth century, many societies denied women citizenship, an education, civil or legal rights. Women in the United States were not allowed to vote until 1920.

This kind of discrimination was even more prevalent in Jesus' day. A woman in Palestine had the legal status of slave or animal. Only the husband had the right of divorce and he could turn his wife out of the home for almost any reason of displeasure. C.S. Cowles in "In Praise of Women Preachers" elaborates:

> Jewish literature is full of expressions of joy over the birth of a son and sorrow over the birth of a daughter. The Genesis commentary called the "Rabbah," written by the Rabbis, describes women as "greedy, eavesdroppers, lazy, jealous, querulous, and garrulous." Rabbi Hillel, grandfather to Gamaliel, taught that wherever women gathered together there was much witchcraft. A good Pharisee prayed, "O God, I thank thee that thou didst not create me a Gentile, a dog or a woman." (2)

Consider the joy felt by Jewish as well as Gentile women when Jesus addressed them with dignity and allowed them to sit and listen to his teaching. Women who had been barred from the inner courts of the Temple and synagogue worship were encouraged to draw near and receive the truth. A few of those women who had served Christ and faithfully stood by to watch the crucifixion were the first to receive and spread the good news of the Resurrection. Later, the book of Acts and Paul's letters indicate that women such as Philip's daughters, Prisca and Phoebe, played key roles in spreading the salvation story (Acts 21:7-9; Rom. 16:1-5).

The right of women to continue to pass on the Gospel, however, was later curtailed by influential Church Fathers. By the middle of the second century, Tertullian offered these principles regarding a woman's role in worship. "It is not permitted for a woman to speak in the church, nor is it permitted for her to teach, nor to baptize, nor to offer [the Eucharist], nor to claim for herself a share in any masculine function—not to mention any priestly office" (Pagels 72).

This patriarchal stance was most likely adopted to help spread the Gospel without causing additional social upheaval. It was also used to combat heresies, such as Gnosticism, that often supported women in ministry but also denied that Jesus was a real human being. Regardless of the reason, most women were prohibited from preaching and leadership positions in the Church for the next 1700 years. It was not until the American holiness movement that any sustained challenge to sexual discrimination against women in the church was launched. Unfortunately, the positive strides toward ministry equality in holiness denominations have been recently hampered by the following reaction.

3. *A backlash to the Women's Liberation Movement of the 1960s-70s:* Outspoken conservative evangelical leaders have blamed most of the ills afflicting families today on a radical feminism that emerged in the last three decades. The feminists who sought equal rights for women in the workplace, were blamed for encouraging women to seek educational and professional fulfillment outside of the home. Many conservatives deplored this movement toward financial and emotional independence, claiming that it undermined "traditional family values."

Is it fair, however, to link all or most of today's family pressures with "women's lib"? Is the woman the only parent responsible for maintaining a loving, nurturing environment for raising children? Is it possible to model before children a Christlike partnership in which husbands and wives share responsibilities according to their gifts and availability?

I am so thankful that this kind of mutual servanthood was modeled by my parents. For my father, spiritual headship involved respecting my mother by listening to her, affirming her efforts to grow and serving her in any needed task (including monotonous housework).

This partnership in the home was exemplified in the church by many holiness churches at the turn of the century. More than 20 percent of the Church of the Nazarene's first pastors, evangelists and missionaries were ordained women (*Manual* 904.10). That percentage has dramatically dropped, however, as many church officials have distanced themselves from the women's rights movement and embraced a "safe stance of silence." Many leaders do not condemn women in ordained ministry, nor do they actively promote women in ordained ministry. It is the hot topic few district superintendents want to address because many female as well as male church members are leery about a woman preaching or a woman leading. As a result, some young women seeking a senior pastorate (or staff position other than children's ministry) face a lonely, often discouraging journey. Even if they are prepared and extremely capable, few churches will consider (much less hire) them for roles traditionally offered to men.

How can the church reverse this discriminatory trend? To recapture a tradition that embraces all humanity on the same level of grace and equips all believers to serve to the fullest of their potential, church leaders should engage in the following three steps:.

1. *Reexamine the texts used to justify discrimination against women in the church.* How can Paul acknowledge women praying and prophesying in the Church in 1 Corinthians 11: 5 without one word of condemnation, and then in 14:34 tell them to keep silent? How could the women, whom Paul warmly commended in Romans 16, continue their public ministry "in silence"?

In light of Paul's overall positive attitude toward women in the Church, (note his commendations of women in Acts 18: 24-26; Rom. 16:1, 6, 12) his command for silence appears to be in response to a specific problem in Corinth. That issue probably was noisy disruption of worship by women. Those who had been denied access to the Scriptures were abusing their newfound freedom to receive and speak truth.

In 1 Timothy 2:11-15, Paul restates an injunction against women speaking in Church. He adds, "I do not allow a woman to teach or exercise authority over a man" (NIV). The rationale given for this prohibition is the "order of creation" of Rabbinical tradition. Man has preeminence over the woman because he was created first. This traditionalist view, however, is countered by Paul in 1 Corinthians 11:11-12 when he states that ". . . in the Lord woman is not independent of man or man independent of woman. For just as woman came from man, so man comes through woman." In other words, after the first Adam, every man would originate from a woman. "In the Lord," one is not above the other.

A second reason Paul seems to bar women from leadership is offered in 1 Timothy 2:14. Since "the woman being quite deceived, fell into transgression," she cannot be trusted with teaching. In Romans 5:12-14, however, Paul contends that Adam, and not Eve, is responsible for the entrance of sin into the world. Paul neither mentions or blames Eve for sin.

Again, the passages used to limit a woman's ministerial role in the church must be seen in light of both Jesus' and Paul's teaching elsewhere. They also must be seen in their proper historical context. It is imperative that we carefully study the conditions that prompted the author to issue these directives.

2. *Reexamine the biblical texts that seem to justify ministerial equality.* On the day of Pentecost, Peter preached from Joel's prophecy that says "your sons and your daughters shall prophesy," and "upon both men and

women, I will in those days pour forth of My Spirit, and they shall prophesy" (proclaim, preach) (Acts 2:17-19). These verses indicate the outpouring of the Holy Spirit issued a new age of ministerial equality.

Paul seems to confirm this in his first letter to the Corinthians by making no distinction between men and women regarding the exercise of spiritual gifts. He writes "to each is given the manifestation of the Spirit for the common good" (1 Cor. 12:7). Limiting a woman's range of expression when it comes to her God-given gifts cannot promote the common good, but only divide and impair the Church. Instead, men and women should rejoice with Paul that in Christ "there is no longer Jew or Greek, there is not longer slave or free, there is no longer male and female; for all of you are one in Christ Jesus" (Gal. 3:28).

In response to this emancipating passage, nineteenth-century preacher Luther Lee exclaimed:

> In the Church of which Christ is the only head, males and females possess equal rights and privileges. . . . To make a distinction in the church of Jesus Christ, between males and females, purely on the ground of sex is virtually to strike this text from the sacred volume, for it affirms that in Christ there is no difference between males and females, that they are all one in regard to the gospel of the grace of God. (80-81)

3. *Educate believers about our Wesleyan tradition that promotes women in ministry.* John Wesley originally argued strongly against allowing women to preach. However, through the influence of his gifted mother, Susanna, the rising need for more lay preachers, and God's apparent anointing on several women speakers, he began to change his mind. He described Mary Fletcher's preaching as "fire, conveying both light and heat to all that heard her" (Roberts 59).

Adam Clarke, biblical scholar and close Wesley associate, concurred with the promotion of women in ministry. "Under the blessed spirit of Christianity, they have equal rights, equal privileges and equal blessing, and let me add, they are equally useful" (Roberts 59).

More than 100 years later, J.B. Chapman, General Superintendent of the Church of the Nazarene, defended the young denomination's positive stance on women preachers. "The fact is that God calls men and women to preach the gospel, and when He does so call them, they should gladly obey Him and members of the church and of the ministry should encourage and help them in the fulfillment of their task" (5).

With or without this encouragement, many women stepped out of their traditional roles in the home to obey God's call to preach. Among them are the following:

Susan Norris Fitkin, an ordained preacher who organized the Women's Foreign Missionary Society to help finance Nazarene missions work throughout the world;

Olive Winchester, a dynamic professor of biblical literature and administrator at two Nazarene colleges; and

Leona Gardner who preached for forty years in the jungle villages of South America.

All three struggled with their Call, knowing that it was often deemed inappropriate by their families and communities. All three courageously heeded their Call by speaking wherever and whenever they could for the glory of God (Laird).

Their ministries, along with the contributions of countless women in a variety of denominations are an inspiration to women today, who must not hinge their obedience on the church's formal sanction. Women who are called to preach and lead must remain faithful to the Caller.

Our faithfulness must also be coupled with Christlike love for our opponents. Rather than nursing bitterness over sexual discrimination, we must prayerfully ask God for grace to forgive and to make the most of present opportunities to serve the Kingdom. We must also be thankful for the slow but steady progress some denominations are making to provide support for women in ministry. Newsletters and conferences such as the "Come To the Water" gathering of more than 500 clergywomen in Wesleyan/Holiness churches provide a rich pool of ministry resources and mutual affirmation. With pure hearts, sound scriptural defense of our ministry and a loving desire to serve, women can help reach countless souls for Christ.

History has proven the effectiveness of women pastors, evangelists and missionaries. Now, more than ever, the church must not deny, but embrace this rich tradition of women working as partners in ministry to carry out the Great Commission.

WORKS CITED

The Bible. New International Version.

Chapman, James Blaine. "October Gleanings." *Herald of Holiness.* 15 Oct. 1930:5.

Cowles, C. S. "In Praise of Women Preachers." Lecture. Northwest Nazarene College, Nampa, ID, 9 May 1991.

Laird, Rebecca. *The First Generation of Ordained Women in the Church of the Nazarene.* Kansas City, MO: Nazarene, 1993.

Lee, Luther. *Woman's Right to Preach the Gospel.* Chicago: Holrad, 1975.

Manual: Church of the Nazarene. Kansas City, MO: Nazarene, 1980.

Morrow, Thomas M. *Early Methodist Women.* London: Epworth P, 1967.

Pagels, Elaine. *The Gnostic Gospels.* New York: Random, 1981.

Roberts, B. T. *Ordaining Women.* Rochester, NY: Earnest Christian, 1891.

Metcalf, Janine T., *M.Div. Rev. Metcalf teaches ministry and Christian education courses at Point Loma Nazarene College, drawing from 13 years as a full-time evangelist and associate pastor in the Church of the Nazarene. A Nazarene ordained elder, she speaks in interdenominational retreats and conferences throughout the United States. She is working on a doctorate at Asbury Theological Seminary.*

CHAPTER ELEVEN

MINISTRY PARTNERSHIP IN THE HOME AND CHURCH

Vicki Copp and Dan Copp

There is no uniform cookie-cutter mold for the type of person God calls into full-time ministry. The stereotypical model of a tall, deep-voiced pastor/husband/father, along with the regal, piano-playing pastor's wife/full-time mother and 2.5 ideally-behaved children is only one of many examples in the pastorate. Today's preachers and church leaders also include single adults, wives who are assisted by their husbands in secular vocations, and wives and husbands assuming pastoral roles together. The latter model typifies our personal ministerial journey today.

Dan is the senior pastor of the 1,000-member Mission Valley Church of the Nazarene in San Diego. Vicki is the senior pastor's wife, the pastor for Bible studies ministries and a candidate for ordination in the Church of the Nazarene. Ours is a partnership in marriage and ministry that is built on two solid principles: Obedience to God and commitment to each other.

As a couple, our sojourn of spiritual obedience began at Point Loma Nazarene College. Dan was a pre-law major who began to perceive God's calling to preach. He conferred with several professors for advice. Their counsel was consistent: "Draw as close to God as you can, and then move ahead to do what you sense you ought to do." Following prayerful reflection, Dan decided he would continue to pursue law until God's calling became more pronounced.

After our marriage, we moved to Sacramento where we helped with teens at Dan's home church. While at an Nazarene Youth International convention, we heard General Superintendent Charles Strickland speak on being clay in the potter's hand (Jer 18:6). When he called for commitments at the conclusion of the message, both of us responded. We knew God had placed a call on our lives. For Dan, it was a call to pastoral ministry. For Vicki, it was a call to be his partner, despite some initial reservations.

Vicki was raised in a parsonage. Even though she experienced many memorable times as a "PK," she carried some insecurities concerning the financial pressures her family had faced. After having carefully avoided religion majors in college, she found herself married to a man with a call to preach! God beckoned her to surrender her anxieties and trust for a fulfilling future.

Our trust level was tested when we accepted a pastorate in Oakland, California. This church had seen wonderful days in the past. The building sat up in the hills of Oakland with a fabulous panoramic view of the Oakland/San Francisco Bay area. The sanctuary could seat 500 people, but the actual attendance on our first Sunday was 56. We were told by those attending that it was the largest attendance they had seen in quite awhile. Most of our mentors and friends at Nazarene Theological Seminary in Kansas City sincerely counseled us against moving to Oakland First Church. It seemed as if everyone but God told us not to go, but both of us felt that it was God's will for us at this time. Those years had their ups and downs, but we held steady because we knew we were there by divine appointment.

One Sunday morning, after we had moved to the San Diego Mission Valley Church, Vicki began to sense her own call to preach. Neither of us understood this, but we wanted to be obedient. We decided to take it one step at a time. Vicki began to discern confirmation of her call as she read God's Word. She noticed new sensitivities in her spirit. She faced a public declaration of her call when General Superintendent Ray Hurn invited those who had a call to preach and had not yet started the ordination process to come forward at District Assembly. For both of us, it was a big step as what had been a quiet, personal call became public. Vicki was especially concerned with how the people of Mission Valley would feel about it. Again, God confirmed the call with the congratulations of church delegates and the District leadership.

Vicki's preparation was our next step of obedience. She began a Master's degree in Theology at Point Loma Nazarene College. God then led her to apply for local and district licenses. The church board officially voted to recognize Vicki as an unsalaried part-time member of the pastoral staff, and left it to Dan and his senior staff to shape her role and implement the board's action. Dan's sensitivity to possible misunderstandings prompted him to move ahead with just the official church board recognition of her ministry. There was no public recognition of Vicki's new assignment, no bulletin or newsletter announcements, and really no broad congregational awareness that Vicki was now one of our pastors.

As Vicki began to minister from an official board-recognized position, she realized that she was having trouble making the adjustment from the role of a layperson to the pastoral role. What we had thought would be a very sensible and sensitive way to accomplish her goal of ordination began to pose a problem. Vicki found that she was not able to minister as a pastor when she was not perceived as one. After conferring with his senior staff, Dan decided that Vicki needed a more visible role in order to minister effectively as a pastor. This process for Vicki was a step of obedience for a more serious, involved role when she could have gotten by with a superficial kind of fulfillment of her requirement for ordination. For Dan, it was obedience in a potentially risky situation involving his wife and her visibility.

When Dan does a wedding ceremony, he normally includes the idea of the marriage being a covenant with God. He illustrates it with the idea of a triangle. Each participant in the covenant is represented by a point of the triangle: God, husband, wife. As the marriage partners move closer to God, they move closer to each other. We have found this principle to be true in our own experience. As each of us has made obedience to God the priority in our lives, we have drawn closer to each other.

With all the stresses of ministry, one dare not add an unhealthy marriage relationship to the mix. Even the positive aspects of ministry can cause division as one partner is in the "limelight" while another is working in the background. One partner can be so enamored with the congregation's need for their services that the other partner and family are slighted. The negative aspects can cause division as the stress, long hours and financial hardship take their toll. There must be a strong core of commitment to the partnership and the family if the ministry is to have long-term productivity for the Kingdom.

As in any relationship, "ministry-partnership" success depends on good communication. We were helped tremendously by a Marriage Enrichment seminar we attended during our years at Nazarene Theological Seminary. We learned skills that helped us communicate to each other in a non-threatening, but direct way.

This commitment to mutual honesty has helped us weather numerous trials. One of our most trying seasons was the year Vicki gave birth to premature twin girls who did not survive. Even though we dealt with the loss in our own ways, we offered each other space and permission to express our pain. Our shared grief facilitated spiritual and relational growth.

Our commitment to each other is also reflected in the way we talk to each other about the ministry. There can only be so much indiscriminate "dumping." We can overwhelm each other with too much information about people's criticisms or problems. We can set up harmful patterns by complaining about our circumstances or situations. We must consider the readiness of the partner to hear what we have to say and the impact our words will have on their perceptions about people and situations. The Holy Spirit offers wisdom as we seek when and how to share.

There is nothing like having the one you love most tell you that you did a great job. We have tried to steadily encourage each other. When Vicki's role has relegated her to the background, Dan has helped her see how important her unseen role is to the partnership. When Dan has led a meeting or preached a sermon, Vicki has been available for affirmation and constructive suggestions.

We also try to help each other meet our personal goals. While Dan completes his Doctor of Ministry program, Vicki takes up the slack at church and at home with the children. While Vicki continues work on her Master's degree, Dan takes over some of the childcare. We both make financial sacrifices to help each other do what we feel we need to do.

When we arrived at Mission Valley with our baby girls—Mackenzie, 23 months and Megan, 5 months—Dan told the board that his family came before the church. They were pleased at that, but were still surprised when he found a replacement for a Wednesday night prayer meeting because he needed to stay home with a sick child, and Vicki was directing the choir. It would be easy to convince ourselves that we are so needed that we must not let our family get in the way. We must protect some time for our families or we may lose them. Our congregations will understand if we take the time to explain to them. They may even offer to help.

We made the decision to have Vicki as the primary caregiver for our girls. This childcare was initially joyfully participated in by Vicki, but with the second child, she began to feel she had no time to call her own. She and Dan decided to have a sitter come in a few hours each week so that Vicki could have some time for herself. It was amazing how that time away from the babies renewed her strength and helped her have a healthier perspective.

Throughout our marriage we have learned that we must protect our relationship. We often set time aside to get away with one another. It is a time to dream, reflect and renew our commitment. With all the needs of people around us, it is easy to put our own needs on the back burner. Giving ourselves time alone helps protect us against the moral failure we hear about so often. Dan has his prayer partners pray for his moral strength and faithfulness along with other areas. He reminds them that besides being a pastor, he is also a human being with human weaknesses. There are practical things that can be done to protect our marriages. Jerry Jenkins in his book, *Hedges,* has many helpful suggestions.

When children come along, our commitment to each other expands to the family. We have made a heroic effort to be at soccer and softball games, at school parties and field trips, and to take time to do things just as a family. We have coached, umpired, directed, accompanied, driven, led, sponsored, participated, and spent. We think our girls know how important they are to us. We hope they grow up with a love for our church and not resentment concerning its intrusion on our family life.

Sometimes our zeal for ministry can cause us to push those who mean the most to us aside. It may provide us freedom to minister initially, but in the long run, we are much less productive for the Kingdom and are certainly cutting ourselves off from the growth and nurture that intimate relationships can provide.

Regardless of where God leads us, we must remember that those to whom we minister watch our marriage and family life. Sometimes we are placed on a pedestal. Other times we are misunderstood or prejudged. No matter how we are perceived, we know we are called to ministry together. Ours is a partnership that is nurtured by God's love and a growing desire to help each other become all we are meant to be.

SUGGESTED READING

Dobson, James. *What Wives Wish Their Husbands Knew About Women*. Wheaton, IL: Tyndale, 1975.

Jenkins, Jerry B. *Hedges: Loving Your Marriage Enough to Protect It*. Brentwood, TN: Wolgemuth & Hyatt, 1989.

MacDonald, Gail. *High Call, High Privilege*. Wheaton, IL: Tyndale, 1985.

Mains, Karen Burton. *Open Heart, Open Home*. La Habra, CA: David C. Cook, 1976.

Senter, Ruth. *So You're the Pastor's Wife*. Grand Rapids, MI: Zondervan, 1979.

Tucker, Ruth A. *First Ladies of the Parish: Historical Portraits of Pastors' Wives*. Grand Rapids, MI: Zondervan, 1988.

Copp, Vicki, *B.A. Ms. Copp has assisted her husband in the pastorate in a variety of teaching, preaching, and worship leading capacities. Answering a call to preach, she is completing a Master of Arts degree at Point Loma Nazarene College as well as the requirements for ordination in the Church of the Nazarene (to be completed in Spring 1997).*

Copp, Daniel, *M.Div. Rev. Copp is the Senior Pastor of Mission Valley Church of the Nazarene in San Diego. He and his wife Vicki have served 15 years in pastoral ministry. While serving on several district and college boards, Dan is completing a Doctor of Ministry degree at Fuller Theological Seminary.*

PART THREE

CONNECTING WITH GOD'S WORLD IN MINISTRY TODAY

*W*hile ministers are called to influence the world, there is no doubt the world powerfully influences ministers. This section examines why pastoral ministry is considered one of the most intellectually, morally and spiritually demanding vocations possible. It explores the tension that emerges when pastors try to reach unbelievers with marketing strategies and therapeutic "feel good" messages and still remain true to the Gospel of repentance and redemption. The authority to speak for God comes from a lifestyle of worship to God plus intimate engagement with God's people and their deepest needs.

CHAPTER TWELVE

WHAT'S AT STAKE: FUTURE OPTIONS FOR MINISTRY

John Wright

The Christian ministry today is one of the most intellectually, morally, and spiritually rigorous vocations possible.Yet it is also a vocation constantly prone to sentimentality. As a matter of fact, to speak of rigor and ministry together seems oxymoronic. Religion in America has become largely therapeutic: religion is supposed to help the individual cope with the demands made by the impersonal, rigorous world around us. If ministry helps to save people from rigor, how can it be rigorous itself? Indeed, ministers have even developed a whole language of piety to mask the rigor and issues that one encounters—"It's hard out there, but God is good, isn't He?" A pious phrase can obscure a multitude of problems. "Well, praise the Lord, anyway."

It seems to me that pious sentimentality presents the biggest danger to Christian ministry today. Sentimentality protects ministers from having to ask hard questions that lie at the heart of the Christian faith and ministry. For instance, why is it that the classical Christian doctrine of the Trinity seems so irrelevant, far removed from the practical functioning of ministry? Inquiring minds should want to know.

Above all, pious sentimentality insulates the minister from having to ask hard questions about the relationship between the church and the world. How much do we shape our ministry in order to correspond to the structures, values, and language produced by our society? How much do we shape our ministry to correspond to the distinct structures, values, and language produced by the Scriptures and the Christian tradition? Which has shaped us most? Which should drive our ministry?

These are not easy questions, nor new ones. The theological issue of the relationship between the Church and the world is not unique to our day. Ministry takes place in history; the Church has always struggled with its relationship to the "world" and always responded in diverse manners. Yet today the church has achieved a certain sociological sophistication that permits an intentional accommodation between the Church and the society. Pious language then masks the profound theological changes such an accommodation entails. Massive shifts in the understanding of ministry have occurred which now impact all who engage in ministry, ordained or lay. Perhaps a little rigorous analysis might prove beneficial as the church approaches the twenty-first century. The "world," it seems to me, presents itself to the church in the religious market dynamics in which all ministry occurs.

The Market Dynamics of Contemporary Ministry

There are very real factors that every minister, lay or ordained, must face today: in America, if not the world, the Christian ministry occurs in an unregulated, free-market religious environment. No governmental or ecclesiastical institutions ultimately determine what may or may not be said, done, or believed in ministry. No official credentialing agency tells the public who the legitimate ministers are. No one may force another into the sphere of her ministry. No tithing member is under obligation to one specific congregation or theological tradition. No one criterion of theological truth exists that determines if a practice is properly Christian or not. Market factors influence the practice of the church.

This situation, it seems to me, has resulted in certain characteristic practices of Christian ministry today. First, and maybe most important, American Christian ministry has been very monolithic in its hoped-for outcomes. This monolithic quality, however, is not to be confused with orthodoxy, of which Americans have always been suspicious. The American religious market has been very monolithic in its consistent desire for personal therapeutic religious experience. American Christian ministry has shaped its practice to meet the market demands set by the culture. Indeed, when a movement has historically moved away from this individualistic experiential focus, it has usually been met with a loss of market share in America.

This leads to a second characteristic: contemporary American Christian ministry concentrates on issues of style, not content. To put it bluntly, the public does not really care what theological tradition one speaks from. As a matter of fact, to speak from a particular theological tradition is suspect, for it is not faithfulness to a tradition, but personal experience that really counts.

Denominationalism is dying in America today because theological traditions have largely become suspect. The market has demanded the same product be supplied wherever religious services are offered; the brand name has become unimportant. That is not to say all differences have been erased. No, different American groups have different experiential backgrounds dependent on demographics such as age, income, and race. Therefore, ministry has become quite sophisticated in stylistically tapping into these demographic pools to invoke the personal experience that is the center of American religion. With the same content assumed every-where, style becomes the only way to differentiate between ministries.

Third, the market dynamics of American Christian ministry have focused Christian ministry on the perceived needs of the potential cus-tomer. One popular and influential pastor has stated Christian ministry is essentially about how one might "find a need and fill it." An undergradu-ate coed at a Christian liberal arts college decides to stop going to classes so that she can "minister" to her dorm—help her sisters through the strug-gles of college life. While Americans may have no innate desire for the gospel, we are awash with perceived needs, desires, and wants implanted within us by the mass culture in which we live. Christian ministry as prac-ticed usually embraces these needs as bridges until the consumer encoun-ters the religious experience that lies at the center of American religion. The market, not a specific theological tradition, determines the precise practices of ministry.

Finally, as in any market system, a clinching characteristic of American Christian ministry is its ultimate pragmatic evaluation. If market share is growing, if individual religious experience is occurring, if the minister's style is "clicking" with his or her chosen market niche, if perceived needs are being met, the ministry is legitimate—"blessed," so we say, by God. Dwelling within a free market economy of individual religious desire, the bottom line remains the same as in any business: market share and profit margin.

Whether these market dynamics are embraced or rejected, they provide the context in which we minister. One may celebrate or bemoan the situa-tion; nevertheless it exists. People today want entrepreneurial leaders who manage well and counsel effectively. Ministerial training, therefore, like any market-oriented activity bears the mark of a "profession" which requires the empowering of students to compete well in the system by initi-ating them into the dynamics of the marketplace. Traditional theological disciplines (i.e., learning the biblical languages) seem strangely irrele-vant—indeed they are, in that context. Yet, despite the academic training of those who minister, as in business, it is often the intuitive practitioner that succeeds best. What Harvard MBA could have competed with Sam Walton or Bill Gates in establishing the market share now possessed by Walmart and Microsoft?

Again, one may celebrate or bemoan the situation, but it seems to me that this is the context in which we minister and begin to fulfill our call. Such a situation, however, exacts a toll on those who minister. First, min-istry has become fiercely competitive. Congregations constantly battle to maintain members. Some win, but as in any free market situation, many more lose. Large corporations (megachurches) can meet more needs, often leaving the smaller churches bereft of the membership and lay lead-ership that support the clergy. Meanwhile, more and more ministry has shifted from local congregations to specialized "ministries." In a competitive environment, the local church no longer is necessarily the primary matrix for practicing the Christian faith.

The fallout in clergy self-esteem has become devastating. Clergy and lay leadership come in droves to hear the marketing wisdom of the latest success stories, only to find the dynamics unchanged in their own church. Lay leaders decide that a minister's style is not to their liking anymore, that they desire to reach a new, younger market; the mature clergy is suddenly "demoted" to a smaller, rural congregation, or worse—left without a charge. On the other hand, clergy ride their "success" in one market for a "promotion" to a larger, more lucrative congregation. Lay leaders who have invested themselves in the clergy's leadership are suddenly left alone, facing the demands of the church by themselves. Market dynamics do not breed vocational or congregational security. The ministry, lay and ordained, has become a very lonely, frightening place.

Even when successful, ministers (lay and ordained) experience the symptoms of such a system. Christian ministry has become a "helping profession." Ministers are expected to operate at low cost, and be constantly available "support persons," meeting the insatiable therapeutic needs of their "clients." Indeed, personal affability and warmness is the characteristic people want most in a minister. Above all else, the minister must be "nice," even when dealing with the most distorted personality. The constant smile, however, becomes difficult, if not immoral, to maintain while constantly encountering the degradation and tragic consequences of the fallenness of humanity, both outside, and maybe especially inside the local congregation. Ministry in this setting tends to consume an individual; an effective lay minister will find more and more responsibility falling upon her shoulders, until finally the burden becomes more than one can bear.

Finally, the free market dynamics empty the minister of any authority. Given that a minister, either lay or ordained, provides a "service" to a group of people with specific needs, authority lies in the customer. The twenty-year old son of the third generation member will often bear more theological authority than the pastor, regardless of how his claims relate to the Christian tradition. Even though his family has held the congregation "hostage" for twenty years, he knows what the community "needs."

With nothing to stand on outside the perceptions of the latest market trends (which the congregation may or may not want to embrace), the clergy's and lay leader's authority is only a function of her or his rhetorical persuasiveness, ability to tap into a new market, or manipulative organizational skills to move the congregation in a new direction without rocking the boat too much. (It is a dangerous business to alienate one's regular customers!) Change within a congregation becomes a major issue. To move a congregation in a new direction becomes a contest between the market vision of the pastor and the lay leadership and the settled environment of the congregation. Authority again becomes pragmatic: what are the outcomes in terms of present and future markets? Contemporary ministry has some deeply entrenched systemic problems.

These problems, however, have deep theological roots. First and foremost, the Christian tradition believes that the customer is not king; Jesus is. The "customer" is a sinner, existing in a fallen, sinful world, and in the process, contributing to the misery that results from sin. From the perspective of the Christian tradition, the problem is not that people have needs, but that people do not know their true need—the healing of their sinful nature through the re-creative work of God in Christ and the Church.

Authority in ministry does not lie in the lay leadership, nor in the pastor's (or pastoral staff's) subjective "vision" for the church. Authority lies in the Scriptures and the Christian tradition that brings us to repentance and reconciliation. The minister speaks to the marketplace of desire to represent the Church of Jesus Christ, calling the world into a new life which redefines what the needs are. Left to the demands of the market, ministry merely legitimates what the society already is experiencing, usually to the society's own detriment. Thus those in ministry are accountable chiefly to the saints who have gone before and the Scriptures that continue to form their lives. Ministry (lay and ordained) takes authority from this accountability, not from the perceived needs of their clients.

When the Christian tradition sees humans as sinners in need of God's redemption rather than customers who set the terms of their own redemption, it places ministers in tension with the culture. Authority, Scripture, tradition, the saints who have gone before, are all concepts difficult to grasp for Americans who desire immediacy with God. Such concepts are just not very therapeutic; they do not necessarily make us "feel better" about ourselves at all. But the fact of the matter is that, while there are therapeutic aspects of God's grace, the task of ministry involves a commitment to truthfulness that is not exactly "therapeutic."

Ministry: The Meeting of Church and World

These are the circumstances today, it seems to me, in which God is calling people to minister. These circumstances present a theological issue that every minister must confront, consciously or unconsciously: What is the relationship between the Church and the world? Is ministry engaging the market culture, meeting needs while pointing to Christ as the ultimate need-meeter? Or is ministry scorning the needs produced by the world in order to form an alternative community of Jesus Christ? Are other options available? The nature of ministry demands an answer. Ministry is where the Church meets the world one way or another. Sentimentality will not do. Only rigorous and faithful theological discernment will suffice.

Ministry models that engage the market dynamics of our culture abound. Yet if we understand that ministry is not primarily to meet human needs but to lead a particular people to worship Christ in all things, contemporary models become more scarce. They do exist, however. Perhaps one will find such models in church history. One thing for sure, new models will arise only if someone is willing to speak truthfully that Jesus of Nazareth, crucified, buried, and raised from the dead, is Lord.

From this perspective, ministry becomes discovering where God takes the minister and the church as we witness together that God has revealed God's own very Self, not in a personal experience, but in Jesus Christ. Ministry unfolds itself as an adventure rather than a technique. Stepping into the religious marketplace and living out the reality that the Kingdom of God has drawn near in Jesus, the minister seeks to live faithfully to the One who has called her or him. Maps and models of ministry, therefore, cannot chart an individual's or community's path, but they can "chart out" fundamental options as one seeks to live as a faithful minister, priest and servant of Jesus Christ.

SUGGESTED READING

Bellah, Robert N. et al. *Habits of the Heart: Individualism and Commitment in American Life.* New York: Harper, 1985.

Finke, Roger and Rodney Starke. *The Churching of America, 1776-1990: Winners and Losers in Our Religious Economy.* New Brunswick, NJ: Rutgers U, 1992.

Goff, Philip K. "Spiritual Enrichment and the Bull Market: Balancing the Books of American Religious History." *Religious Studies Review* 22.2 (1996):106-112.

Hauerwas, Stanley and William H. Willimon. *Resident Aliens: Life in the Christian Colony.* Nashville: Abingdon, 1989.

Moore, R. Laurence. *Selling God: American Religion in the Marketplace of Culture.* New York: Oxford UP, 1994.

Wells, David F. *No Place for Truth: Or Whatever Happened to Evangelical Theology?* Grand Rapids, MI: Eerdmans, 1993.

Wright, John, *Ph.D. Dr. Wright is an Associate Professor of Religion at Point Loma Nazarene College. In addition to his Bible, theology, church history and ministry courses, he is the Director of Summer Ministries, with responsibilities for student interns in churches throughout the southwest. Before coming to PLNC, Wright taught at the University of Notre Dame, where he received his Doctor of Philosophy* *in theology degree and pastored two Nazarene churches in Indiana. He has authored or co-written four books and has numerous articles in biblical and theological journals.*

CHAPTER THIRTEEN

WHAT IS AUTHENTIC WORSHIP?

Randall Davey

Twenty-one year old Eric Darr reluctantly attended Holy Week services at Christ's Cathedral with his elderly grandfather on the condition that his grandfather would attend Easter services with him at Community Fellowship. Eric and Grandpa Merritt slipped quietly into the Gothic style church, past a greeter who whispered, "Welcome," and sat in an old varnished pew. Grandpa reverently knelt on the kneeler and bowed his head while Eric suspiciously eyed the architecture.

The organist, who was nowhere to be seen, played a selection that Eric did not recognize. Without invitation, the congregation stood, the choir processional began and several persons in robes walked down the center aisle. The minister said a few words and then the congregation responded in unison. Eric said nothing but did follow along in the worship book his grandfather extended for him to see.

Eric scanned the crowd as the majority seemed engrossed in reading prayers or hearing Scripture lessons and occasionally singing a few lines of something. Fortunately, the sermon was brief but not memorable. Communion followed and on the hour, the service was dismissed.

On the way to Eric's house, Grandpa said, "Well?"

"Well what?" Eric answered.

"What did you think?" the old man asked.

"Not much. I didn't get a thing out of it," Eric offered in a disapproving tone.

On Easter Sunday morning Eric proudly escorted his grandfather into a large, nondescript auditorium. Mr. Merritt noted the basketball hoops on both ends of the "sanctinasium." Though the service was not slated to start for another thirty minutes, a band accompanied five young and similarly dressed men and women who held microphones close to their mouths while loudly belting out repetitive lyrics. As the congregation gathered, they waved to each other and clapped to the beat of the music. At 11:00 a.m. sharp, a neatly dressed man, sporting dress slacks and a turtleneck, strolled to center stage and shouted, "Arise, church, and sing!" Mr. Merritt obediently looked for a hymnal that was not to be found. The words of the choruses were displayed on the wall high above and behind the platform singers. Sing they did. For twenty minutes, they sang and clapped and sang and clapped. Sometimes they sat and sometimes they stood and Grandpa Merritt thought to him-

self that this service afforded more aerobic activity than his "seniorcize" class at the Y.

When the singing ended, casually dressed Pastor Jim moved from the audience to the platform and shared for twenty minutes, after which a drama team "acted out" the application of the sermon. Pastor Jim assured visitors that nothing done this morning was intended to offend them, that he hoped they were comfortable enough to come back and to feel free not to participate in the offering.

It took Eric and Mr. Merritt an hour to exit from the crowded parking lot. It had been a banner day for Community Fellowship and Eric was beaming.

"Well?" Eric said with eyebrows raised.

"Well, that was surely something," Mr. Merritt said. "It was surely something."

Which service came closest to being authentic worship? What a loaded question! To suggest that one of these two services is more authentic than the other is inflammatory and divisive for they represent the current polarization of worship practices in the evangelical community. Still, the question begs an answer so it is important to find some ways to satisfactorily work with it. What are possible starting points?

1. *One can start with one's experience and one's reasoning.* People often choose churches that remind them of their "home church." There tends to be an underlying assumption that the church where one comes to Christ or the church where one has the largest store of positive spiritual memories somehow did things the right way. Out of gratitude for a goodly heritage, all other religious experiences are weighed against the backdrop of one's upbringing. In this instance, authentic worship is worship that parrots that with which one is most familiar.

   A different twist on the same point occurs when one participates in a church very different from one's upbringing but equally positive, if not more so. This is especially true if one attends a rapidly growing church or large church and either the novelty or genuine difference is so impressive that the new church becomes the standard by which other churches are evaluated. Here, people reason that if the church is large or growing, "they must be doing something right." Maybe they are and maybe they are not. Regardless, authentic worship is "as the new church does."

2. *An appeal to tradition may be another way to work with the question.* Admittedly, tradition is more than one's experience of tradition. If one can move beyond that restriction, consider how the church has understood the call to worship for the last fifty years before tackling the last five hundred years. Not that long ago, denominational distinctives were clearly apparent and similarly expressed in worship practice around the world. Now, in the broader evangelical community and not to the exclusion of nineteenth-century holiness folks, worship is more

generic and transdenominational if not a-denominational. While many conservative churches have continued to delineate particular ethical ways to express one's faith, worship practice tends to be locally determined with little consideration of the shorter or longer tradition of Christ's church. This is not to say that everything done for centuries is right. It is to say that one would do well to at least understand why the church did what it did and practiced what it practiced for centuries before uncritically latching on to a new trend.

3. *If experience, reason and tradition are an insufficient trio of criteria, consider the Scriptures.* The Scriptures certainly are not a last resort. Rather, they should be a starting point but they tend not to be. One is inclined to start with and be fascinated by one's experience, reason and tradition, arguing, "if it was good enough for Dad, it's good enough for me and if anyone's in heaven, it's my dad." Those kinds of summary statements translate to this. "Don't confuse me with Scripture." "My mind is made up."

What happens when one appeals to Scripture to settle the question of what is authentic worship and what is not? Interestingly, the Bible does not provide an order of service. Does it provide the Ten Commandments? Yes. Does it give us the Beatitudes? Yes. Does it present orders of service? No.

What the Bible does, however, is provide several "glimpses" or impressions of that which constitutes worship historically, as well as in the life to come. It is safe to say that biblical worship includes elements of praise, giving God glory, singing, confessions and/or creeds, Scriptures read and explained, prayers, offerings and sacraments. (Some suggested passages to support this are Ps. 2:11, Ps. 95:6, Ps. 47:1, Ps. 134:1-2, Ps. 141:2, Neh. 8:6, Hab. 2:20, Matt. 26:26-8, Heb. 12:28-29, Heb. 13:15-16, Luke 4:16-21, John 4:24, Rev. 1:12-17, Rev. 4:2-11, Rev. 5:13, and Rev. 19:5-7.) One can quickly see that list of components will not help significantly with the question of authenticity in worship. Perhaps another question will.

What is at the Heart of Authentic Worship?

Worship is a focused God-humankind encounter of grace. It defies understanding that the Holy Creator of the universe, revealed in the person of Jesus, would want continued intimate relationships with those who apart from his intervention are Hell-inclined if not Hell-bound. While God extends a holy invitation to relationship, he calls for a holy response. While methods and style cannot guarantee a divine encounter, worship experiences may help or impede the probability that those who seek him will find him. How can one planning worship services assist pilgrims in worship?

Is it a question of focus? Some students of the evangelical community and the holiness movement have argued that neither group emphasized worship. The evangelicals concentrated on evangelizing and holiness-folk concentrated on leading persons into the experience of heart holiness. Accordingly, everything else in the service was subservient to the end results. Service components were included or excluded on the basis of how they would help or hinder results. During the past century, worship hymns and anthems were replaced with gospel tunes, designed intentionally to aid the evangelist. Worship services were blended with and ultimately became synonymous with evangelistic services.

It was not a terribly big leap from this concern to a preoccupation with sociological categories as determinants for worship practice. Church growth writers give due attention to baby boomers, baby busters and especially the likes and dislikes of "unchurched Harry and Mary."

To attract the unchurched or reach the bored and apathetic church attender, worship planners unwittingly can drift into an entertainment-based service that is more fun than not, more lively than boring where folks feel like they get their "money's worth." Real concern is consistently demonstrated for how unchurched folk feel about irritating words like "the Cross," "sin," "repentance" and the like. The results speak for themselves. Some of the fastest growing churches are "seeker sensitive" churches. Does that mean that the question of authentic worship has been settled? I think that is hardly the case. The data simply suggests that some churches do a better job of attracting persons predisposed to attend church than others. It does not say much about what happens once they are there.

While the Bible does not detail an order of service, it does underscore the "worth-ship" of God, the subject and object of worship. That which is done is to be done "unto Him," versus unto the congregation. From time to time, congregations respond to special selections of music by applauding, perhaps giving rise to the impression that the musical offering was a performance for the pleasure of the congregation. Only the offerer of the music knows for whom the selection is intended, but for it to be worship of God, it must be offered to him with a clean heart for his glory. When worship planners purpose to glorify God from prelude to postlude, evangelism is the byproduct versus the goal of the service.

The longer tradition of the Church offers some items for consideration. How can one assist persons in the encounter of the Holy Other in worship? Here are a few elements which deserve a closer look:

- *Prelude:* What is the purpose of the prelude? Some use it as a musical announcement indicating that the worship service is about to begin. In that setting, one is more likely hearing a musical preliminary.

Others see the prelude as time to prepare for worship. Worshippers have been preoccupied with the concerns of work and play, relationships, the secular and inane; now they gather to worship. It is a tough transition to go from banal chatter or significant conversation to the worship of God. Preludes can be unfamiliar tunes, symbolizing the incomprehensibility of God or they can be familiar melodies, encouraging worshippers to turn toward God in spirit.

- *The Call To Worship:* All kinds of community groups start club meetings with song. That does not mean all kinds of community groups worship. The minister has a privileged role in inviting the gathered community to the focused privilege of worship. "The call" can be scriptural, sung or spoken but specific in purpose. A word about musical selection here applies to the whole service. It is possible for some music to trivialize the mighty acts of God. The tunes and lyrics should correspond to the One revealed in the life, ministry, death and resurrection of Jesus.

- *Response:* Having been invited to worship, the congregation responds with an act of God-centered worship. While this is frequently a hymn or chorus, it may be unison-reading of Scripture. This point is equally important. *Worship is primarily done by the people, not for the people.* Participation is key.

- *Invocation:* Having offered God worship, one stands uniquely with brothers and sisters in the Presence of the Holy One of Israel, acknowledging his Presence. In that Holy Presence, one can be moved to prayers of invitation, thanksgiving and confession as well as the Lord's Prayer. In those prayers, one asks something of Him. One may seek his face, his Presence, his grace, his forgiveness for a word ill-spoken or for deeds done or left undone. His Holiness demands accountability before we can really worship in spirit and truth.

- *Honor Him:* It is always appropriate to express thanks and to honor God for answering prayers. There are myriad ways to "glorify" Him, which is agreeably the chief end of the human race. The creeds are invaluable as well, in shaping the character of the confessors.

- *The Word:* In an age where there is notable biblical illiteracy, the public reading of the Word is vital. It may be the only Scripture to which persons are exposed all week long. In a day where sound bytes are cherished, "some Word" is better than "no Word," but one may want to utilize a resource designed for a very similar time centuries ago when folks either could not or did not read the Word. The lectionary was an intentional and systematic approach to exposing persons to the full counsel of the Word. Contemporary lectionaries provide recommended Scripture readings which correspond to the Christian calendar. Here, the word can be both read and proclaimed after which the congregation may be called to response in prayer.

- *Offerings:* One pastor said, "Now the ushers will take the collection." It would be more appropriate to invite those who have heard the Word and bathed in grace to express thanks in a material way as well by giving of means to the Lord. It is a high point of worship to invite persons who are tempted to believe that they are "self-made" to praise God from whom all blessings flow.

- *Celebration of the Lord's Supper:* Long before the altar call was a popular addendum to worship services, the church relied on the Lord's Supper as a desperately needed means of grace by which all who gathered could respond to the preached Word. The more modern altar service implies there are many, if not the vast majority, who hear the Word but have no need of responding. The sacramental supper, on the other hand, is an opportunity for all to respond to the Christ who suffered, died, and was raised in their behalf; the Christ who is so very present and the Christ who will come again. Jesus instructed the disciples to observe this meal that never loses significance for the believer who dares "to remember" and believe (Luke 22:14-20). While the "altar call" is a late development in the life of the church, the communion of saints at table is rich in biblical tradition.

- *Dismissal:* Just as Jesus sent the disciples into the world, the pastor is privileged to disperse the church to do the work of ministry to the glory of God. It would be quite fitting to add a crisp announcement about which the community needs to be informed before praying a prayer of benediction upon them.

It is not unusual for persons to cower at the very thought of a liturgically sensitive service. "Too formal." "Looks Catholic." "No room for the Spirit." It is not about formal or informal. It is not about freedom or bondage. Worshippers can give meaning and life to form. Obviously, there is no inherent value in dead form even in the guise of spontaneity.

Authentic worship is a gift of God to the people of God, a celebration of relationship with Him made possible in Christ. It is a heart-felt expression of gratitude to Christ Jesus for His redeeming work. It is the glorification of One who will come again to receive those who believe unto Himself. It deserves deep thought, critical reflection, careful planning done in a spirit of humility and reverence. Worship that truly focuses on God will never be insensitive to believers or seekers alike.

SUGGESTED READING

White, James F. *Introduction to Christian Worship.* Nashville, TN: Abingdon, 1990.

Liesch, Barry. *People in the Presence of God.* Grand Rapids, MI: Ministers Resources Library, 1988.

Webber, Robert. *Worship is a Verb.* Waco, TX: Word, 1985

Davey, Randall, *M.Div. Rev. Davey serves as Senior Pastor of Fairview Village Church of the Nazarene in Pennsylvania. He has pastored churches in Ohio, Kansas and Pennsylvania for 19 years and has done extensive research on the significant role of worship in congregations. Davey has been an adjunct professor at MidAmerica Nazarene College, as well as a monthly contributor to* Bread *magazine.*

CHAPTER FOURTEEN

INCARNATION IN THE NEIGHBORHOOD

Steve Rodeheaver

It was two Sundays before Christmas, and we were on our way home from church. This particular Sunday we were giving a ride home to Gabriella and her three brothers. Gabriella is a nine year-old Mexican-American girl who lives just over a mile from the church. Her three brothers are ages fourteen, twelve, and seven. They have been involved in the church for the past couple of years through various outreach ministries. As of late, Gabriella and her brothers have been quite regular in attending our Friday night Bible school and meal ministry. They have even made it on a few Sundays. Because their ability to attend is so sporadic and they have no phone, we do not pick them up for church. However, we do let them know that any time they make it to church, we will see to it that they get a ride home. That is what happened on this Sunday. Gabriella and her brothers walked to church and we were giving them a ride home.

Gabriella's family is fatherless. While there is no way to measure the full impact of their father's absence, one definite result is poverty. Gabriella's mother is on a government-subsidized fixed income, trying to raise four children in one of the cruelest parts of the city. They live in a cul-de-sac backed by thirty-foot canyon walls. Dope is smoked openly on the sidewalks. Gang tags are everywhere. Drug dealers try to wave you into the alley behind the liquor store as you approach their street. Crack, heroine, and crystal are all available. Turning onto their street one is overwhelmed with the sensation that there is no way out. It is as if you are behind enemy lines. You sit in your car fearing what could happen to you and hoping that it will not. You pray, and then you marvel. Somehow, Gabriella and her brothers escape to church and the church shows up on their street. Both are completely unimaginable, except by the Spirit.

The Point Loma Nazarene College Early Childhood Development Center annually adopts a family during November and December with the dual purpose of teaching children to share as well as to provide a Thanksgiving dinner and some Christmas presents to a needy family. They asked us if we knew of a family that they could adopt. Knowing they could really use the help, we suggested Gabriella and her family to them. The week before Thanksgiving I had the privilege of dropping off a turkey, ham, and all the trimmings to Gabriella's mother. She and the kids were over-

joyed by the scene of all the food. A few weeks later, on a Friday night, I had the privilege of dropping off Christmas presents to Gabriella and her family. Talk about excitement! You would have thought that Santa himself showed up. I knew that the wrapping did not stand a chance, but I told them to wait until Christmas before they opened their presents. I think I made it about as far as my van before I heard the paper tearing.

That next Sunday Gabriella and her brothers came to church and we were giving them a ride home after the service. Though it was still two Sundays before Christmas, the kids had opened their presents from the Early Childhood Center. Gabriella's brothers were gleefully telling us all about what they had received. Out of the blue Gabriella started a side conversation with my wife, Vonda. I will never forget her opening words: "Vonda, my mother has started drinking again." The conversation was short, maybe a sentence or two by each one. We were soon past the drug dealers and in front of Gabriella's house. There was not much to say except that we would be praying for her and that we hoped to see her next Friday. Gabriella and her brothers got out of the van and went to play with their presents.

As we drove on home I could not get away from Gabriella's words about her mother. I was not surprised that she was drinking; I already knew that she struggled with crystal. Gabriella spoke the words so matter-of-factly that I am not sure she was even surprised. Yet Gabriella's message/cry was stunning. It came just two days after I had delivered their presents. It was glaringly obvious that the presents, though quite nice, had not met the need. Christmas was still two Sundays off and then some.

Gabriella's pain has raised afresh a crucial question in ministry: *What do we do when the gifts do not match the needs?* Though not always so acutely as on that ride home, it is an issue that we deal with constantly. The needs of our neighborhood go far beyond our abilities and resources. Even outside resources, while they are of great help, still come up short. From the cries of children to the confusion and rage of teens to the despair of adults to the bewilderment of grandmothers and the loneliness of the well-aged, the hurts of people are so deep and their lives and circumstances so complex that ministry often seems a farce. What presents are we going to drop off two weeks before Christmas that are going to bring peace and wellness when Mom has started drinking again? There is no escaping this issue. It stretches from the inner city to the wealthiest of suburbs to the most remote country towns. Human pain is unfathomably deep and everywhere. So what do we do when the presents we seek to give are woefully inadequate?

It seems to me that the answer lies not in more and greater presents, but in *presence*. While Gabriella greatly enjoyed her present, her pain yet required the presence of an ear, the attention of a heart, the shoulder of a friend, and the assurance that she was not walking this frightful path alone. Vonda, through her presence, gave her what the present could not.

Too often we operate out of a "present" view of ministry as opposed to one of *presence*. It is easy to treat sermons, food, clothing, lessons, music, Bible studies, etc., as presents that we bring to people in hope of meeting their needs. While these presents are good and worthy gifts which God often uses to bless people, they are not enough in the dark, often lonely, hours of life. Present-centered ministries are void of meaningful relationships, and thus come up short in the face of existential need. In the dark hours of life we need not only a sermon, but also a pastor; not only a meal, but also one who will sit at table with us; not only a lesson, but also one who is living it among us; not only a song, but also a choir in which to sing. In a ministry of presence, we do not just give gifts, we give ourselves. As we give of ourselves, over time, relationships are built and established. In the context of these relationships life-sustaining ministry takes place.

Jim Scharn, a colleague in ministry, once told me that people will not remember much of what I say, but they will remember me—who I am, how I follow Jesus, the priorities I live, how I treated them. He was right. We are remembered for the giving (or not giving) of ourselves. Jim was not saying that solid preaching and teaching are unimportant, only that people remember the preacher better than the sermon.

Presence ministry is based on the way God ministers to us. God does not remain aloof in heaven, safely removed from the human predicament. He does not try to save us from above. Instead, "the Word became flesh and dwelt among us, and we beheld his glory, glory as of the only begotten from the Father, full of grace and truth" (John 1:14 NASB). In the phrasing of Eugene Peterson, "The Word became flesh and blood and moved into the neighborhood . . ." (185). In Jesus, God moves into our neighborhood. He comes to meet us where we are, to live with us in the depths of our needs. Several gospel narratives come to mind: the woman at the well; the death of Lazarus; Zacchaeus; the man possessed by a Legion of demons; etc.; but especially the baptism of Jesus. There Jesus, the one who is sinless, gets in line with a bunch of sinners to be baptized a "baptism of repentance for the forgiveness of sins" (Mark 1:4 NIV). He who knew no sin stood in line identifying himself with sinners. He was with them in their deepest need. This was but a preview of his cross, his baptism of death on behalf of sinful humankind. He so moved into our neighborhood that he bore the curse of our sin. *That is presence.*

Along with moving into our neighborhood to stand with us and for us, the Word became flesh to reveal the Father to us. "No one has ever seen God, but the only begotten, who is at the Father's side, has made him known" (John 1:18 NIV). It is in the coming of Jesus that God makes himself known. We cannot know God except when he moves into our neighborhood. (We cannot move into his.) He moves in precisely to reveal himself that we might know him and receive him. The cross is the pinnacle of God's self-revelation. There we see the heights of his holiness and the depths of his love. His heart is laid bare in the blood of Jesus. Risking rejection, he makes himself known that we might receive him. *That is presence.*

God never intended his ministry of presence to come to an end with the ascension of Jesus. Rather, through the giving of the Spirit of Jesus, his intent is to have an even greater presence localized in more than just one person. We are to carry on his *ministry of presence,* moving into neighborhoods, standing with and for hurting people, revealing the heart of God. Jesus tells us that "he who receives whomever I send receives Me; and he who receives Me receives Him who sent Me" (John 13:20 NASB). It is truly incredible. We, the disciples of Jesus, become the tangible presence of God in the world. Whoever receives us as we live out our discipleship actually receives the One we follow and serve. God's presence to the world is in and through us.

"Whoever receives you receives Me." How can they receive us if we are not there? We have to be present in order to be received. We have a great desire for people to receive Jesus, but too often we are not willing to be a presence representing him. We move out of neighborhoods whose ethnicities are different from us and then raise money for cross-cultural missionary work around the world. We are willing to give presents, but we are not willing to be present. For disciples of one who was present with Samaritans, lepers, tax collectors, the dispossessed and the possessed, we are a strangely absent people. For people to receive Jesus, there must be the presence of Jesus' disciples.

It is tempting to try to establish a ministry of presence without really being present. We are with people, in the name of Jesus, but we are not willing to be authentic. We put a mask on our humanness seeking to avoid vulnerableness. We dare not let our own weaknesses, failures, and shortcomings show. We have to be strong and on top of everything, both to protect ourselves and represent Jesus well. We forget that Jesus was human. We forget that he got tired, thirsty, worn down, hungry, angry, grieved and tempted. We forget that Jesus had to get away and pray. We forget that while Jesus sometimes concealed his divinity, he never hid his humanity. If people are going to receive Jesus, they need to be able to receive us, and they cannot receive us unless we are genuinely us.

As we seek to follow Jesus and live authentically in the neighborhood, presence begins to be established and relationships start to form. As people receive us into their lives they receive Jesus as well. The conversion process is taking place. Ministry is happening. Through our obedient presence neighbors are discovering that God is present, that he is with them and that he loves them. Sometimes his divinity is concealed, but through us he lives before them his ways and his values. They begin to believe in and know him for themselves.

"My mother started drinking again."

"We'll see you Friday."

Maybe not the end-all solution to the problem, but a promise that means more than a gift. Maybe not all that Gabriella hopes and longs for, but the presence of one representing her only hope.

Blessed are you who will be present, for in your presence you will become peacemakers. You will not solve all the world's problems—you probably will not stop Gabriella's mom from drinking (but then neither would all the gifts in the world). Instead, in your presence you will bring a touch of peace to those who are in turmoil, a bit of wellness and health to those who are hurting, and some righteousness and justice to both those who are doing wrong and those being done wrong. As you give of yourself you will impart value and meaning to those whom you serve. Your presence will make a difference. Indeed, those who receive you will receive the Life himself. And you will be called sons and daughters of the God who becomes flesh and moves into neighborhoods.

In no way is the above emphasis on a *ministry of presence* to be read as a de-emphasis on a *ministry of proclamation*. While there will be moment-by-moment decisions as to which form of ministry is most appropriate for a specific situation, ultimately there is no choice. Biblical ministry mandates both proclamation and presence. The two go hand in hand. It was the Word that became present.

There is an argument being popularized today that denies the power of words. Those who create violent and degrading songs, television shows, movies, videos, etc., allege that their words have no creative power, that they do not influence or persuade society to act in like ways, that they are only expressing what already is. From heavy metal bands to rap groups, from the producers of raunchy television shows to the directors of R-rated movies, there is constant and consistent denial of responsibility for the direction that our culture is moving. Words are just words, so they say, and beliefs and behaviors cannot be traced to them. After all, "sticks and stones may break my bones, but words will never hurt me."

The "word industry" betrays its true position—that words are all powerful in shaping desires and directions—in two significant ways. First, consider the whole realm of advertising. If words have such little power to influence, why do so many companies spend billions of dollars in advertising? Clearly there is the belief that if they come up with the right words they can persuade the consumer to choose their product over the competitor's. Running behind every commercial is the conviction that a word, heard clearly enough and often enough, will influence our thinking and our choices. We buy the word before we buy the product.

A second clue to how the industry truly feels about words is found in the cultural issues it "explores." Whether it is *Murphy Brown's* right to have a child, or the legitimacy of a lesbian marriage on *Friends*, or the appropriateness of "viewer discretion advised" shows like *NYPD Blue*, merely addressing those issues betrays an underlying perspective. What is the purpose of communicating a perspective? At the very least, to create understanding and acceptance, but at the heart, to persuade adoption of and adherence to the same perspective.

Words are indeed powerful. We suspected it when the name-calling of our siblings and friends hurt us as much or more than the sticks and stones. We are convinced of it when we consider the investments made in the media (both news and entertainment) to shape our perspectives and decisions—even while denying the power of mere words to do such persuasive work. Thus, we are bombarded by words as people and institutions and corporations seek to mold us. And yes, you are being bombarded right now. This very book exists because of the belief in the power of words to shape you.

So far we have been talking about human words. If our words have such force and impact, imagine the power and authority in God's words. The first thing we learn upon opening our Bibles is that God's word is creative. By that I do not mean that God speaks creatively (although He certainly does). Rather, God creates by speaking. I remember my granddad talking with me about creation when I was a boy as we walked about his farm. Wanting to impress him with how much I knew, I told him that God could have created it all with just his little finger. I have not forgotten his response: "God did not use his hands, not even one little finger. He spoke the world into creation." It was by his word that God created the heavens and the earth and all that is in them. His word brought the universe into being.

The theme of God's creative word runs throughout the Bible. Isaac was born because God had given a word, a promise, to old Abraham and barren Sarah. The Hebrew's exodus from Egypt was rooted in the divine words, "Let my people go." Israel was on a journey to the *promised* land. God continued to speak to his people through his prophets. Listen to the word to Jeremiah: "Then the Lord reached out his hand and touched my mouth and said to me, 'Now, I have put my words in your mouth. See, today I appoint you over nations and kingdoms to uproot and tear down, to destroy and overthrow, to build and to plant'"(1:9-10 NIV). Jeremiah was not given an army nor any kind of advanced technological secrets for such a task, but only a word from above. God did not just create the universe by his word, but all of history, and most significantly, salvation.

In the New Testament the power of the divine word is seen throughout Jesus' ministry. It only took his word to calm the sea, still the wind, heal the sick, cast out demons, forgive sins, and raise the dead. The disciples, as well as everyone else, were constantly marveling at the authority and creative power of Jesus' words. There had never been a teacher like him, whose very words could impart life.

Jesus not only brought the word from above, he was the word from above. Jesus did not just proclaim the gospel news that the Kingdom of

God was at hand, he was the gospel news. Thus, the early church proclaimed the creative word of Jesus to all who would listen. Those who listened and believed found themselves to be involved in a new creation: "the old has gone, the new has come." The gospel word of Jesus was life-giving. It was and is the power of God. Hear the words of Paul to the Corinthians:

> For the message of the cross is foolishness to those who are perishing, but to us who are being saved it is the power of God. For it is written: "I will destroy the wisdom of the wise; the intelligence of the intelligent I will frustrate." Where is the wise man? Where is the scholar? Where is the philosopher of this age? Has not God made foolish the wisdom of the world? For since in the wisdom of God the world through its wisdom did not know him, God was pleased through the foolishness of what was preached to save those who believe. Jews demand miraculous signs and Greeks look for wisdom, but we preach Christ crucified; a stumbling block to Jews and foolishness to Gentiles, but to those whom God has called, both Jews and Greeks, Christ the power of God and the wisdom of God. (I Cor. 1:18-24 NIV)

Notice two things: First, the word of the cross is a divine word among a world of human words, and all words, whether divine or human, have the same intention of persuading belief, perspective, and commitment. There is no neutral word. Either one's mind is being renewed by the divine word or human words are squeezing the mind into earthly thought-molds.

Second, while there are many words, there is only one word from above, and although it may sound foolish in comparison with these other words, it is the only word with saving power. In the proclamation of the word of the cross—Christ crucified—God is at work destroying the words of mortals and creating life in those who believe. Every argument is taken captive by the foolishness of the gospel.

The *proclamation* of God's word is essential to creating life and combating the words of death. A life-giving ministry is a ministry that speaks the gospel. God's word is the only word that creates hope, perseverance, purity, second chances, forgiveness, love, and holiness. There is no other word that saves. It must be spoken. The people need to hear it. The minister needs to hear it. As in Genesis 1, it will not return null and void. We have the assurance that God will continue his creative work as his word is proclaimed.

Again, *presence* and *proclamation* go hand in hand. If the Christian community only proclaims the word without being present in the neighborhood, the word will go unheard. It needs to be spoken from a place where people can hear it. (In truth, it is already unheard by the very ones proclaiming it, for the word calls for presence.) At the same time, if there is presence without proclamation, the ministry will be weaponless in its battle with the world and its many words. Proclamation is essential to the creation of new life from above. The dead in the neighborhood need to hear the gospel word in order to come to life. The living in the believing community need to hear the gospel word in order to live and receive power to continue the ministry of presence.

Where there is no proclamation, presence will die. Where there is no presence, proclamation has yet to be heard. Where there is both proclamation and presence, creation of new life is taking place.

WORKS CITED

The Bible. New International Version.

The New American Standard Bible. Le Habra, CA: Lockman Foundation, 1960.

Peterson, Eugene. *The Message.* Colorado Springs: Navpress, 1993.

SUGGESTED READING

The Bible (seriously!!!)

Brueggemann, Walter. *Finally Comes the Poet.* Minneapolis: Fortress, 1989.

Nouwen, Henri. *In the Name of Jesus.* New York: Crossroad, 1989.

—. *The Wounded Healer.* New York: Doubleday, 1972.

Peterson, Eugene. *Working the Angles.* Grand Rapids, MI: Eerdmans, 1987.

***Rodeheaver, Steve,** M.Div. Rev. Rodeheaver has served for nine years as Senior Pastor of San Diego's Southeast Church of the Nazarene, an intercity ministry in a multi-cultural neighborhood. He is an adjunct professor at Point Loma Nazarene College in the Department of Philosophy and Religion and was named a President's Ministerial Fellow in 1995.*

CHAPTER FIFTEEN

MINISTRY AND LEADERSHIP WITH SHORT TERM MISSIONS

Dana Walling

S *itting atop a rickety scaffolding constructed of poles cut from the nearby forest, we paused, waiting for the next bucket of mortar to be tied to the rope so we could haul it up and pour it down the holes in the concrete block we had laid. Looking out across the Caribbean, we could see the inevitable thunderstorm brewing on the horizon. In part, we wished for its hasty arrival to give us a respite from the oppressive heat that was stealing the air from every breath. The other part of us was wishing for it to wait until we finished work because we wanted our mortar to set before it came.*

It was a good time for reflection, this pause on a stifling tropical afternoon. It was the second week of a two-week mission trip and the unmet expectations have surfaced. The children have stolen every corner of available heart space and there does not seem to be any more to give. There was a final indignity. I was fighting off waves of dysentery that made a person wonder if it is worth it all.

In this moment of reflection, the coed who has been working tirelessly beside me asks a critical ministry question: "What difference are we making here? I mean, I could quit school now, move to this community and give the rest of my life, but what difference would it make?"

Nearly everyone who has ever experienced the kind of intense ministry that a short term mission experience offers has faced similar questions. Short term missions (STMs) overwhelm you with the immensity of the need. At the same time, they illuminate the puniness of our abilities to effectively meet those needs. We go in response to a call from the Lord to make a difference. And everyone who ever ventures out on a STM discovers the questions that the young college woman was asking on that sweltering Caribbean day. These are the questions that shape the value of the experience and help to shape the person's understanding of ministry.

No one can deny that the last quarter of the twentieth century is a time when the Church of Jesus Christ has been marked by short term missions. In 1970 there were no departments of Work & Witness nor Compassionate Ministries in the Church of the Nazarene. By 1995 those two departments represented the fastest growing areas, producing the greatest amount of resources for the denomination. As Powell indicates in another chapter of this book, this trend represents a return to the biblical values of justice integrated with evangelism.

A growing sense of global community is the major factor contributing to the rise in STMs. Most denominations and church groups have been moving away from colonial models of missiology to internationalization. This opens up the opportunity for resource sharing and ministry understanding in non-traditional ways. Thus the idea of short term involvement to assist the national church has emerged as a popular and effective way of accomplishing the Great Commission.

Other factors contributing to this include relatively inexpensive and rapid travel. Greg Livingstone has calculated that the cost for William Carey to transport his family one way to India in today's dollars would have cost him about $400,000 (17-20). The journey took months in the 1700s, yet today he could purchase round-trip fare for his entire family for less than $10,000 and get there in less than a day. Another factor that explains this explosion of STM activity is the media. Through the modern technology of television and more recently, satellite transmission, we are truly living in McLuhan's "global village." We can learn about what is going on in other countries more quickly. This breeds a sense of community and encourages the desire to personally experience what is happening with our neighbors.

Sociologically, the activism of the Boomer generation has led them to a greater direct involvement in mission activity. Not content to sit back and contribute to missions only with their pocketbooks, they have spawned more activistic types of involvement both in and out of the church. Events like LiveAid, BandAid, Comic Relief, and FarmAid are secular endeavors that are mirrored in the church and parachurch world of STMs. In the field of Youth Ministry, national leaders like Tony Campolo and Ridge Burns have touted the benefits of STMs for intensive impact on young lives. Burns reports that STM experiences were most often cited as the most life-changing events in the young lives in his youth groups. The research of Strommen, Warren, Zuck and Benson and others supports this finding. Benefiel's research cited elsewhere in this volume also records a growing activist minority within the Church of the Nazarene.

The thrust of this chapter is that short term missions, properly done, provide an intensive environment for experiencing and understanding ministry. Some biblical examples of short term mission activity, discussion in greater detail why STMs are valuable to ministry, some keys to a successful STM experience and an analysis of issues in leadership and ministry in connection with STMs are presented.

From the beginning it is important to remember that STMs are not an end in themselves. They are a means of ministry, but ministry should never be defined in terms of an experience or a task. Neither should ministry be defined as an occupational career. "Ministry" is a lifestyle of giving in response to the grace of God one has received. To be sure, some will answer a call that will lead to an occupation of ministry. Yet the vocation of ministry is for all believers.

Short term missions abound in both the Old and New Testaments. Though we are not accustomed to thinking of them in the same way we think of STMs today, the pattern is often the same. A person or group responds to the call of God to go and speak the Word of God to a place that is not their home. The mission usually lasts for a designated period and then they return to their home. In this simplest of models for STMs, it is easy to see that they indeed have biblical precedent.

The paramount example of a short term mission in the Old Testament is the story of Jonah. The prophet was called of God to go to Nineveh and proclaim the need for repentance and revival. His choice of travel accommodations notwithstanding, it was a very successful trip. Jonah's circuitous route to Nineveh is a good example of the need for obedience and sensible planning in response to God's call. If he were alive today, there is no doubt Jonah would wish he had consulted a travel agent. Likewise, an important lesson for all STM participants is to learn to leave the outcome with God. Or, as pioneer STM director Norm Shoemaker, now Senior Minister of San Diego First Church of the Nazarene, is so fond of saying, "Hold all expectations loosely."

In the New Testament we see Jesus on two occasions calling his disciples together and sending them out in teams to minister to the surrounding regions. In both settings, Jesus sets the pattern for evaluation and debriefing as critical components for a successful STM. As Hawthorne points out, Jesus also deliberately led his disciples into a cross-cultural experience for the purpose of breaking down racial barriers with the good news that the gospel is for everyone (27; John 4:1-42 NIV). Jesus set the pattern that was picked up and followed by his disciples. From Phillip's journey to Ethiopia, to Paul's extended missionary journeys, the idea of going out in the name of the Lord was clearly a pattern followed by the Early Church.

Though not all of the Church's missionary work has been conducted with integrity to the Gospel, the idea of short term missionary work to support the ongoing missionary work has always been a part of the strategy of fulfilling the Great Commission. There is a legacy of the past on present day attitudes and underlying reasons for doing STM.

Why Have Short Term Missions? That is a good question that needs to be asked and answered on a regular basis. One of the primary reasons for doing STMs is the intensive impact it has on the lives of those involved. In a STM everything is condensed. There is not much time to waste. If it is done with insight and intentionality, traveling with a team develops an intense level of community quickly. In most cases, STM relationships also develop quickly with the national people.

Another good reason for doing STMs lies in the benefits of leaving one's host culture. Quite often, the kind of reflection that produces new levels of growth cannot take place when you are enmeshed in your host culture. There are too many voices in the clamorous noise of the dominant culture in conflict with the voice of God. Early in the 1990s, I found myself on a bus with 20 United States Christian college students and 20 Brazilians. We had traveled a grueling schedule for eight days, often sleeping on the bus while completing a whirlwind evangelistic tour of the Southern Cone of South America: Brazil, Argentina, Uruguay and Paraguay. There were seven days left and our differences were beginning to penetrate the veneer of our civility.

One young man was along who had a distorted view of ministry. His ideal model for evangelism was to fly into a community, hold a big evangelistic rally, and then leave for the "next gig" having first "counted coup" and notched his evangelistic gunbelt with the number of conversions. This was a concept cultivated in the large megachurch he grew up in and nurtured by American televangelism models. Needless to say, his concept was being severely challenged due to the intimate contact with the Brazilians to whom he found himself captive. In one frustrating moment, he cried out to a young Brazilian friend who was trying his patience, "Don't touch me!" The Brasiliero quickly replied, "I touch you, man! I touch you all the time . . . this is ministry, man!" Laughing, the Brasiliero walked away, but he left an indelible imprint on the young man's life. He was later heard to say, "I failed on this trip. I thought I knew what ministry was, but I had no clue." To his credit, he learned his lesson well. He is a successful youth minister today because he understands what true ministry is. It is a lesson I doubt he would have learned so quickly without the intensive extracultural experience of his STM.

An obvious corollary to leaving our host culture is the benefit derived from encountering another culture. Learning to embrace diversity is a survival skill on a STM. It is not an option. Likewise, on a STM one learns that ministry is grounded in servanthood. Properly done a STM places one at the disposal of either long-term missionaries or national church leaders. Often one is thrust into situations that are less than desirable and doing tasks that are considered menial. Yet if that is what one is assigned to do, then that is what one must do. Ministry perceptions are quickly transformed from up-front performances to more authentic actions of grace and mercy often done in secret.

In short, STMs, properly conducted, become incubators of ministry consciousness. It is here that the participant gets outside her own culture and encounters the wonderful and diverse challenges of true ministry in the name of Jesus. The result is most often a more passionate and compassionate person who has a more realistic view of ministry and an aversion to spiritual quick-fixes. The operative phrase in this paragraph is "properly conducted."

It is the intention of this chapter to delineate the keys to a successful personal experience on a STM. The logistical details for implementing a successful STM program are exhaustive and will be left for others to discuss. This section is most interested in helping the individual maximize the potential for ministry formation through STM participation.

The first key to success is *planning*. The old saying is still true: If you fail to plan, you plan to fail. Planning for your STM involves thinking through when to go, with whom to go, your motivations for going and what you hope to gain from the experience. Such thinking will lead to planning in terms of logistics, physical, mental, emotional and spiritual considerations and goal setting. Having clear goals is the follow-up to your planning. Begin with a vision statement for what you would like to see happen in your life as a result of the trip. Then establish what you need to do to get ready. Finally, identify the steps you will take to get to your goal.

The most important key to your success as a short term missionary is *prayer*. From the moment you decide to go, you should bathe the event in prayer. Pray for personal preparation; pray for the missionaries, the local church leaders, the friends you will make and the people that will be reached by the ministry. Pray for tangibles and intangibles. Mostly, in your prayer, listen hard so that you will allow yourself to be formed more and more into the mind of Christ.

Another key to success in your STM, is to *utilize the three R's of STMs: Reading, wRiting and Reflection.* Your reading should be specific to the culture and language group with whom you will be working. Reading the history of the country and reading the *Internet* listings for the area are also helpful. In addition, read some biographies of missionaries and some devotional classics to nurture your own spiritual growth. By undertaking an intentional reading program designed to open your mind to the country you will visit, you will avoid one of the major weaknesses in today's STMs. Too often, participants in STMs have not learned from an informed reflection on the lessons of the past. Reading about the country and especially its religious, cultural, social, and political history will better equip you to effectively represent the gospel when you go.

One of the mistakes people make in undertaking a STM is to assume that the trip begins when you take off. In reality, your STM experience begins the moment you begin to dream about it. As soon as you plan to go, you should begin to write all your thoughts about it. Journaling is the best friend of your experience. It captures the memories and the things that are most often forgotten after the experience. After prayer, a *journal* of your thoughts before, during and after your experience is a most important key to success.

Reading and journaling are the gateways to reflection. Reflection about what you experience, its connectedness to the reading, your emotions, relationships and spirituality is essential. From the fertile ground of your reflection will come the personal and interpersonal growth which will produce the moments of heightened insight that psychiatrist Gerald May calls a "unitive experience." "Now and then to every human being priceless moments are given in which willfulness stops, spontaneously and without intent. At these times, awareness reflects everything with total clarity and brightness, and one's whole attitude toward life is at least temporarily transformed. Will and spirit become one" (51).

From these moments of transformation a lifestyle of authentic ministry is formed. Add to your personal reflection, the focused reflection of your fellow sojourners and the experience is even more enhanced as you encounter true *koinonia,* the hallmark of the *ecclesia* of Jesus Christ. From this perspective arises the greatest opportunity to learn about leadership in the body of Christ.

Perhaps no topic has received more attention in the twentieth century than the study of leadership. Never has so much been written or spoken about such a loosely-defined topic. Most of the literature assumes an *a priori* definition of leadership exists. Unfortunately, even a cursory reading of the literature indicates that such a universally understood definition does not exist. Although this essay cannot explore the whole range of issues in leadership studies, there are leadership and ministry issues that emerge in a discussion of short term missions.

The definition problems of leadership in general also exist when reading about leadership in ministry. Nearly everyone assumes that ecclesiastical leadership resides in the pastor. While it is clear that ecclesiastical offices have certain authority, it is a mistake to assume that authority is synonymous with leadership. It is also confusing to think of ecclesiastical authority as synonymous with ministry. Just as ministry should not be defined simply in occupational terms, neither should leadership be restricted to ecclesiastical office.

For the purposes of this discussion, the following definition is proposed: *Leadership in ministry occurs when a leader engages other believers to mobilize resources and to utilize the gifts of the Spirit within them to accomplish the mission of Christ in the world.*

The basic assumption of this definition is that leadership in ministry is dynamic. That is, it does not reside in one person indefinitely. It is also relational. There is no such thing as leadership over inanimate objects. One does not lead rocks or pencils. Further, it is irrelevant to discuss any kind of leadership that does not involve humans. One can lead sheep into green pastures, but it can hardly be equated with the decisions George Bush faced when Iraq invaded Kuwait. Yet the leadership involved in any human situation is worth discussing.

To further understand leadership in ministry, one must understand that leadership is tied to accomplishing the mission of Christ in the world. Leadership must have a direction and leadership in ministry is always directed to serve the cause of Christ. Ministry leadership is always servant leadership. Leaders in ministry must recognize the gifts of others and the focused-releasing of those gifts is essential to accomplishing the mission. In reality, the focused-release of gifts is a part of the mission of Christ. Finally, an important function of leadership, especially in ministry, is realizing that available resources are scarce and that the competition for them is intense.

With that definition in mind, short term missions are excellent avenues for developing an understanding of the nature of ministry leadership. Donald Schön writes about the necessity for a leader to do "reflection-in-action," which he describes as, "on-the-spot surfacing, criticizing, restructuring, and testing of intuitive understandings of experienced phenomena; often it takes the form of a reflective conversation with the situation" (42). In a properly conducted STM this is exactly what happens. The forced crises of ministering in a cross-cultural context with a group often results in a development of leadership skills that are later utilized in other ministry contexts. STMs are, by nature, "reflection-in-action" events. Shön also discussed the importance of experiential learning in an organizational environment as forming a basis for later leadership success. STMs provide opportunities for experiential learning in ministry environments which contribute to the overall leadership knowledge base of those involved.

In our experience at Point Loma Nazarene College, a symbiosis exists between the STMs and ministry leadership on campus. Recently, we were looking at a team picture of our first trip to Russia with 53 students from eight Nazarene colleges or universities. Of that number over two-thirds are now involved in or preparing for ministry leadership. Such was not the case prior to the trip. No doubt the "reflection-in-action" of that mission experience had a dynamic impact on the formation of their concept of ministry leadership.

In 1977 Robert Greenleaf gathered his thoughts on organizational leadership and organized them around the theme of *Servant Leadership*. He wrote, "A new moral principle is emerging which holds that the only authority deserving one's allegiance is that which is freely and knowingly granted by the led to the leader in response, and in proportion to, the clearly evident servant stature of the leader" (10).

The connection to STMs should be obvious by now. In a properly conducted STM, the participants learn the value of service. They learn that it is not conditional, nor convenient, nor once undertaken, is it easily abandoned. They also learn the difference between happiness and joy. Having served in decidedly non-tourist conditions in another country, and having connected with local people in the most authentic of human conditions, a joy for serving emerges that most often alters the way a person views the world. That person is no longer content to mindlessly consume the world's resources. That person is no longer given to climbing occupational or economic ladders as ends in themselves. They are the kind of persons who are sensitive to the needs of others around them. They are the kind of people who do not wait until all the training is completed, or the degree is conferred or until the ceremony of laying-on of hands for ordination is over. They roll up their sleeves and serve the needs that they encounter in the world with joy. In so doing, they will be followed and they will be more comfortable in leading. It has been said that he leads least who seeks only to lead, to which I add she leads best who only seeks to serve. These are the lessons of leadership learned in a short term mission.

In summary, short term missions have been shown to provide an intensive environment for experiencing and understanding ministry as well as developing leadership. It reminds me of an experience I had in seminary.

Sitting in a class on youth ministry, we were discussing a successful youth ministry model with the youth pastor and youth staff of a local church. Having been in youth ministry full- time for about six years at that point, I was in a deep discussion with one of the youth staff of the church. We were talking about the challenges of discipling junior highs and the value of missions trips in that process. It was one of the most stimulating discussions I had in my seminary career. Most of my classmates did not understand the concepts we were discussing because they had not been involved in ministry with youth at that level. Some of them were studying to be ministers, and they had not even so much as taught a Sunday School class or attended a Church Board meeting, much less participated in a cross-cultural ministry experience. Yet, in a matter of months, some were going to be in positions that required leadership in a local church. Even more amazing was the fact that the youth staff person with whom I was discussing deep concerns of discipling junior high students was an eighteen year-old high school student.

What is wrong with this picture? I believe it illuminates two very distinct and conflicting concepts of ministry. It is safe to assume that everyone in that seminary classroom felt called to ministry. The difference lay in their concepts of the nature of ministry and the means by which one pursues ministry. For one group, ministry was a profession. For the other group, it was a lifestyle. For the former, the path to ministry meant taking a religion major in college, completing a seminary degree and entering the workforce in much the same way a business major might complete college and pursue an MBA before entering the marketplace of employment.

The professional mentality results in an attitude that ministry is something you do. You prepare as best you can and then you do the ministry. When you have done the work of ministry, you go home or go on with the business of living your life. At that time the seminary had every student

148

complete a practical experience program. Ostensibly every seminarian was supposed to be involved in a local church. At some churches in the area, however, the pastor would simply conduct a class with the seminary students in which he would gather them all in his office and regale them with stories of what it was like in the ministry. No doubt the students gained some valuable lessons from the pastor's ministry travelogue, but they still did not have actual ministry experience.

In a world where we tend to measure our lives by the experiences we have, it is easy to view ministry as an experience. It is equally easy to consider ministry as an occupation. In truth, it is neither and both at the same time. Short term mission experiences have a place in preparation for a life of ministry. They are intense cross-cultural experiences that get one out of a comfort zone and into a place where radical discipleship is demanded. Yet STMs, while beneficial, are not the essence of ministry. Real ministry demands academic preparation, intense practical experience, reflection-in-action and a commitment to faithful service wherever one is placed by God. It is just as valid in the suburbs as it is in the city streets; just as meaningful in the halls of academe as it is in the remotest village in the rain forest. One should never equate a part as the whole. Ministry is rooted in serving humanity in obedience to Christ and it should be measured across a lifetime and not in three-week intervals. The intense experiences of a short term mission exist to serve the formation and development of a lifetime of ministry. To that end, everyone should experience a short term mission trip.

WORKS CITED

Burns, Ridge. *The Complete Student Missions Handbook.* Grand Rapids, MI: Zondervan, 1990.

Campolo, Anthony. *Ideas For Social Action.* El Cajon, CA: Youth Specialties, 1983.

Greenleaf, Robert K. *Servant Leadership.* New York: Paulist P, 1977.

Hawthorne, Steven C. "Not Thirsty, Still Hungry." *Stepping Out: A Guide to Short Term Missions.* Ed. Thomas Gibson et al. Seattle: YWAM Publishing, 1992. 27-32

Livingstone, Greg. "Does it work?" *Stepping Out: A Guide to Short Term Missions.* Ed. Thomas Gibson et al. Seattle: YWAM Publishing, 1992. 17-20.

May, Gerald. *Will And Spirit: A Contemplative Psychology.* San Francisco: Harper and Row, 1982.

Shön, Donald A. "Leadership as 'Reflection-In-Action'." *Leadership and Organizational Culture.* Ed. T. Sergiovanni and J. Corbally. Urbana, IL: U of Illinois P, 1986. 36-63.

Strommen, Merton. *Five Cries Of Youth.* Rev. ed. San Francisco: Harper, 1988.

Warren, Michael, ed. *Youth Ministry: A Book Of Readings.* New York: Paulist P, 1977.

Zuck, Roy B. and Warren S. Benson, eds. *Youth Education and the Church.* Chicago: Moody P, 1978.

*Walling, **Dana**, Ed.D. Dr. Walling is the Executive Director of Spiritual Development at Point Loma Nazarene College. He supervises all student-led campus ministries, conducts weekly worship services and coordinates the college's international mission trips. Walling is also an adjunct professor at the college, teaching undergraduate as well as graduate ministry courses. Before assuming his roles at the college, he pastored in Minnesota, Idaho and Kansas.*

CHAPTER SIXTEEN

COMMITTING CHRISTIANITY IN PUBLIC

Sam Powell

Every minister of the gospel sooner or later encounters such passages as Isaiah 1:16-17:

> Wash yourselves; make yourselves clean; remove the evil of your doings from before my eyes; Cease to do evil, learn to do good; seek justice, rescue the oppressed, defend the orphan, plead for the widow;

and Matthew 23:23:

> Woe to you, scribes and Pharisees, hypocrites! For you tithe mint, dill, and cumin, and have neglected the weightier matters of the law: justice and mercy and faith

and James 1:27:

> Religion that is pure and undefiled before God, the Father, is this: to care for orphans and widows in their distress, and to keep oneself unstained by the world.

How the minister proposes to obey the significance of these passages depends on whether he or she has come to grips with the biblical demand for justice. Sadly, Wesleyans in the past have often attended more diligently to keeping themselves unstained by the world than they have to practicing justice.

What does "justice" mean in the Bible? Although the Bible offers no definition, it provides a portrait of the godly king who acts justly:

> May he judge your people with righteousness, and your poor with justice. . . . May he defend the cause of the poor of the people, give deliverance to the needy, and crush the oppressor (Ps. 72:2,4).

At its most basic level, "justice" is protecting the poor against the rich and powerful. More broadly considered, it designates a condition in which none is able to employ wealth and power unfairly and to the disadvantage of others. It includes speaking for those who cannot speak for themselves and protecting them against the boastful threats of the powerful. So justice is wider than speaking and acting for the poor against the rich; it calls us to side with anyone who is oppressed by those who are more powerful.

We may be tempted to believe that justice is an Old Testament (i.e., obsolete) concept and that there is no concern in the New Testament for fair treatment of the poor. This temptation may arise from the belief, common among American Christians, that Christ's kingdom is a purely spiritual kingdom; from the conviction that the church should not meddle in worldly political affairs; or from the assumption that no righting of wrongs will occur until Christ returns. However, the New Testament itself is not silent on this matter. That Jesus took the plight of the poor with great seriousness is evident from Luke 6:20-25:

> Blessed are you who are poor, for yours is the kingdom of God.
> Blessed are you who are hungry now, for you will be filled. . . .
> Woe to you who are rich, for you have received your consolation.
> Woe to you who are full now, for you will be hungry.

Although concern for the poor and downtrodden is not conspicuous in Paul's letters, it is prominent in the letter of James:

> Come now, you rich people, weep and wail for the miseries that are coming to you. Your riches have rotted, and your clothes are moth-eaten. Your gold and silver have rusted and their rust will be evidence against you, and it will eat your flesh like fire. (5:1-3)

Undoubtedly, justice is a salient theme of the Bible; however, Wesleyans in today's church climate are unlikely to incorporate it into their thinking and ministry unless convinced that the pursuit of justice is consonant with evangelism. This hesitance is due to the fact that Wesleyans commonly consider the church's fundamental (if not sole) obligation to be making disciples. Although we could, on good grounds, regard justice as an essential component of being a disciple, Wesleyans have been inclined since the 1920s to interpret the making of disciples mainly in terms of the numerical growth of church membership. It is relevant to ask, then, how the command to do justice can be harmonized with the Great Commission of Matthew 28. To answer this question a knowledge of the conditions the church faces in the closing years of the twentieth century is necessary.

Today the church of Jesus Christ in the United States faces difficulties of a sort hitherto not encountered. Unlike the persecution in past eras that sought overtly to destroy the church, today's difficulties threaten to thrust it to the sidelines of historical obscurity. On the one hand, the church faces the growing secularism that has emptied European places of worship and that seems on the verge of becoming the actual religion of America. On the other hand, the church faces the daunting task of defending its claims against the appeal of vibrant religious communities like Islam.

What then is evangelism to look like in the twenty-first century? It surely can no longer consist of knocking on doors and waving the Bible at people. Today, when the church's evangelistic task is most pressing, it can least assume a widespread knowledge of and appreciation for the Bible. Nor can the church rely on city-wide revivals—their current ineffectiveness in bringing about first-time conversions is well-known. If the old forms of evangelism are of doubtful value, perhaps the question of evangelism should be rephrased: "What should the church say to the world and how should it say it?" Because America's culture is no longer saturated by biblical images and conceptions, as it was in the past, the form that evangelism takes tomorrow must differ from the form it took yesterday.

The question of evangelism raises the more particular question of apologetics. Apologetics has always been understood as a preparation for evangelism. Apologetics is the church's attempt at countering the objections of unbelievers and at bringing about a sympathetic hearing of the gospel. The church has sometimes in the past assumed that the best way to prepare unbelievers to hear the gospel is to prove the existence of God by means of philosophical proofs and then to demonstrate that the Bible is God's word by means of historical arguments.

Regrettably, this excessively intellectual approach has had only limited success in preparing the way for evangelism. There is no reason to believe it will prove more successful in the future. Yet the need of apology is not thereby nullified—evangelism will not succeed by announcing the Bible to people who do not even know what the Bible is. What is called for today is a different sort of apologetics, one that is not so much a philosophical introduction to the Christian faith as it is the Christian faith itself. That is, the church's best defense against objections and preparation for evangelism is the Christian faith presented in a way that is comprehensible and attractive to unbelievers. But what is this way? Within the church, the Christian faith is commonly conveyed in two forms—preaching and teaching. The apologetics that is called for, however, is a public stating of the same Christian faith but in different forms. Although these different forms may be numerous, there is one that is of particular importance today. That form is the Christian life as shaped by the sound principles of Christian ethics.

Although we may not be accustomed to thinking of the Christian life as a form of the Christian faith, there is ample biblical support for this contention:

Not everyone who says to me, "Lord, Lord," will enter the kingdom of heaven, but only the one who does the will of my Father. (Matt. 7:21)

Thinking rightly about faith requires that we refuse to consider it solely in terms of belief and instead acknowledge its inextricable connection with Christian ethics.

Here we should pause and note that Christian ethics is more than prescriptions regarding individual morality. It is true that the Christian life consists in individual lives lived out in faithfulness to God. However, the Christian life also presupposes theological reflection on the pressing ethical issues of our day. Evangelicals and Wesleyans have made a specialty out of emphasizing individual morality. They never tire of drawing attention to the failure of many Christians to live in a Christian way. However, they have not been as diligent about sustained reflection on matters of public ethics. They have in general been far better at learning the techniques of individual conversion than at thinking hard about the corporate shape of the Christian life. When they have paid attention to ethics, they have managed to make the Christian life seem like a list of prohibitions that pertain strictly to private morality—don't drink, smoke, or dance.

If Christianity is be faithful to God and to accomplish its task of evangelism, it will have to present itself as more than a negative and private morality. It will have to make a case for itself, not mainly in the intellectual sphere, but in the moral and public sphere. Although there is a proper intellectual task of responding to the intellectual attacks of unbelievers, the world will not be won by argument. In short, it will have to show by living examples, both individual and corporate, that Christianity is a meaningful and morally sound life. It must fashion a theology that is directed outward to the non-Christian public.

Such a public theology must be capable of demonstrating that the Christian life is ethically responsible and responsive to the moral issues of our day and it must prove that the central principles of Christianity entail workable solutions to the full range of human problems.

Of course, none of this implies that the church will have the solution to every moral dilemma and that it will supplant civil government as the main avenue of human welfare. The church has a proper task that differs from the work of civil government and it is mistake for the church to seek to become relevant to society by becoming involved in matters that are peripheral to its calling and that other agencies are better prepared to perform. There is no sense in the church attempting to solve social problems that are the province of government and for which government has vaster resources. Nevertheless, the church does have the prophetic task of holding government responsible for performing its task, at least where that task impinges on human welfare.

In summary, unless Christianity is to be progressively relegated to the status of an individualistic religion of pure inwardness and accordingly a church of pure convenience, the church must work at actualizing its historic belief that Christianity is important for human beings as such, not only for human *souls*. It must set forth Christian ethics—in the full sense of the term—as the main form of apologetics, as the most effective form of theology in the public arena.

What forms can justice take? The Christian's duty may be summarized under four points.

First, the church must itself be a model of justice. Regrettably, the church has in the past not only failed at times to act justly, it also has not infrequently sided with the powers of oppression. Instead of speaking for the powerless, it has contributed to their silencing.

The demand that the church become a model of justice suggests that fairness and equity should be the rule in all church dealings, whether between pastor and congregation or between church and community. It also suggests that we should always be alert to the possibility that individuals or even whole classes of people within the church may be subjected to unequal and unfair treatment. A historic example across nearly all of Christianity is the church's treatment of women, to whom the possibilities of professional ministry and church leadership have been and in places are still denied.

By being a model of justice, the church seeks to realize Jesus' command that we let our "light shine before others, so that they may see [our] good works and give glory to [our] Father in heaven" (Matt. 5:16).

Second, Christians have a responsibility to act justly in the world. Here the idea of vocation is required to reinforce the seriousness of this responsibility: every human occupation can be regarded as a service to God when performed in a spirit of obedience and humility. Not only clergy, but also every Christian is called to serve God in the workplace, whether it is located in the home, office or other work site. Because there are no secular occupations, each Christian's livelihood possesses an ethical dimension. Labor is more than an opportunity to provide material goods; it is a means of serving God and neighbor and should be performed in the light of that fact. As a result, even our work outside the church requires the sort of ethical seriousness that clergy devote to the professional ministry. One part of this is justice. Christians should, in their labor, act justly, in the effort to love God with all the heart, soul, mind and strength and to love their neighbor. Anything less than this devotion to justice is a failure to live the Christian faith.

Third, the church has the task of witnessing to the need of justice. No matter how brightly the church's light may shine, the world in its darkness may not perceive it and the church's exemplification of justice. As a result, the church must call the world's attention to its need of justice. Once, in

America, this was an easy task, since virtually everyone attended church. The pastor then had only to preach a stirring sermon and community leaders would have heard the call to justice. Today, however, with a majority of Americans having at best a tenuous connection with the church, other methods are required. By whatever legitimate means, the church should attempt to shape the moral climate of its community so that the question of justice is a matter of public concern. For example, the church should keep the growing gap between rich and poor before the public eye and should continually remind all humanity of its responsibility to use the earth's resources wisely. None of these efforts guarantees that justice will increase; however, the church is called to bear witness to God's commands and to be the voice which, if seldom heeded, at least is often heard.

Fourth, and most difficult and dangerous, the churches should work to increase justice. It is one thing to keep before a community's attention the demand of justice; it is another thing to actively seek to influence the making of laws and their interpretation and execution in such a way that the society actually grows more just. This is the most difficult task because, pertaining to public policy, it requires broad agreement in the church on the specific forms that justice should take: What should the minimum wage be? How may workers best be protected against unsafe working conditions? What is the best welfare policy? It is the most dangerous task because here the church comes close to abandoning its proper task and allowing peripheral tasks to consume its energy. In fact, the church itself as an institution should probably not be directly involved in the formation of legislation. Its job is not to write laws, but rather to remind lawmakers of their responsibility before God. However, the individuals that compose the church can and should be directly involved, in forms ranging from voting, to lobbying efforts, to running for political office.

What may the church expect from its efforts to promote justice? There is no reason to think that injustice will end, that poverty will cease, that wrong and oppression will terminate. However, the Lord of the church states rather clearly that "as you did it to one of the least of these who are members of my family, you did it to me" (Matt. 25:40). In other words, the church's efforts toward justice are a response of faithfulness to God. Those efforts are subject to the ambiguities of history; nevertheless, the church is called to follow the Lord who commanded it to "do what is true" and love "in truth and action" (1 John 1:6 and 3:18).

Note: All scriptural quotations are taken from the New Revised Standard Version.

Powell, Sam, *Ph.D. Dr. Powell currently chairs the Department of Philosophy and Religion at Point Loma Nazarene College. He joined the faculty in 1986 after teaching at Nazarene Theological Seminary, Fullerton College and Rancho Santiago College. Powell also served as a youth pastor at Bloomington (CA) Church of the Nazarene. An accomplished writer, his works include numerous articles for religion journals and two chapters on Christian ethics in a forthcoming book from the Nazarene Publishing House.*

CONCLUSION

"The solution to the problems we encounter in the area of adapting methods to changing circumstances lies in maintaining what Paul called 'a sense of what is vital.'. . . The ultimate ministerial tragedy is to suffer martyrdom for something which really doesn't matter very much anyway." (Purkiser 137)

The goal of *Maps and Models for Ministry* in the twenty-first century has been to acquaint readers with "what really matters" when heeding God's call to a lifetime of service. The contributing authors believe that ministry is much more than a call to a place or paid position. Ministry is a servant lifestyle characterized by Christlike surrender and self-sacrifice. It is the constant willingness to say "yes" to wherever God leads, to whatever God asks, with whomever God chooses. For every divine assignment, regardless of how menial, there can be eternal ramifications. This is what sets ministry apart from all other human endeavors. It is the highest, and at times, hardest of callings that is utterly dependent on our relationship with the Caller. To this end, the book has emphasized the value of personal worship, prayer and serious study of God's Word. In the words of John Henry Jowett, "We are great only as we are God-possessed."

This God-possessed journey is not only meant to be a vertical encounter but also an ongoing horizontal engagement with God's church and world. Ministry has lasting value, only as it is coupled with authentic love and respect for others. This is a love that never sees people as units to be counted, but as precious souls who have been bought with a price beyond measure. It is a love that compels us to affirm the spiritual gifts of all believers and to hold each other accountable to grow in Christ. It is a love that aches over sin, but makes the most of every opportunity to reach sinners with the hope of salvation.

Considering the deep needs of our world and the immense expectations placed on ministers today, it is no wonder that so many feel inadequate for the tasks ahead. This humble awareness of the needs, however, is a prime prerequisite for fruitful ministry. We can rest knowing that God's grace is sufficient to match us for the mission. We can also take heart that

God does not call us to meet all human needs and expectations. This is one reason why countless others have been called and equipped by God for ministry. The authors who contributed to this project attest to this fact. Together, they represent a variety of cultural backgrounds, academic and ministry endeavors.

With hearts poised to receive God's anointing and direction, may our lives be set apart for sacred service. May our thoughts, words and actions echo the commitment captured in the lines of this beautiful hymn:

> Consecrate me now to Thy service, Lord,
>   By the power of grace divine;
> Let my soul look up with a steadfast hope,
>   And my will be lost in Thine.
> (Fanny Crosby, 1875)

Janine Metcalf

WORKS CITED

Purkiser, W. T. *The New Testament Image of the Ministry.* Kansas City, MO: Beacon Hill P, 1969.

Turnbull, Ralph G. *A Minister's Obstacles.* Rev. ed. Westwood: Revell, 1946.